POLSKA

{This book is dedicated to Babcia Ziuta and Babcia Halinka, who instilled in me two passions: food and writing.}

Zuza Zak

POLSKA

NEW POLISH COOKING

photography by
Laura Edwards

quadrille

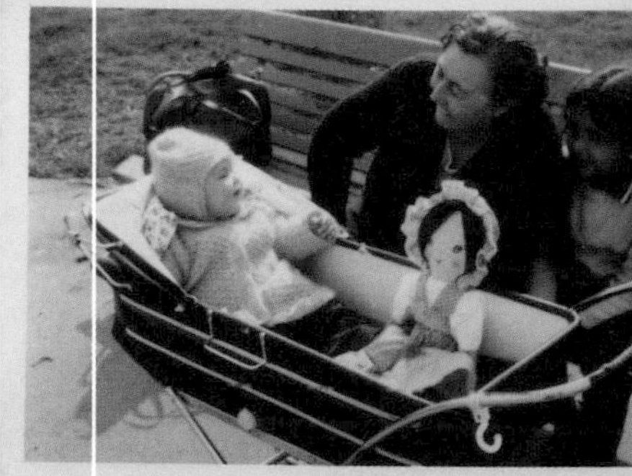

CONTENTS

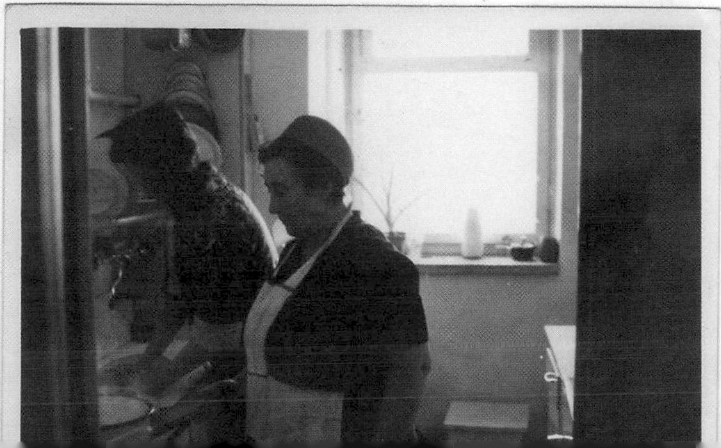

INTRODUCTION

"NAJISTOTNIEJSZA CECHA JEDZENIA JEST JEGO UMIEJSCOWANIE NA GRANICY ŚWIATA NATURY I ŚWIATA KULTURY."

"The most vital attribute of food is its placement precisely on the border between the world of nature and the world of culture."

{Waldemar Żarski, Książka Kucharska Jako Tekst}

To understand a cuisine is to understand a culture. To understand a culture is to understand the spirit of a nation. The word Poland derives from the word 'pole', which means 'field'; so even the name of my country is connected with the earth. We define ourselves through our cuisine, which we love deeply, nurture and continue to uphold. Yet it is misunderstood in many parts of the world. Why? Every minority culture faces prejudice and ignorance, yet I believe Polish cuisine, which I remember so fondly from my childhood, is particularly prone to this kind of misalignment.

The Slavic culture is one of hospitality; most people prefer to eat at home, or at the homes of friends and family, rather than in restaurants, and it is at home where the best food is found. I have explored my childhood memories spent in Poland during the Communist years and I have also delved deep into Polish history books to gain a real insight into my country; to retrieve traditions that have been forgotten; to compare the colourful folklore of the peasantry with the more refined tastes of the aristocracy; focusing on common threads that run through the soul of this ever-changing nation. For this is a cuisine that has survived the partitions, where Poland effectively ceased to exist for over 100 years and when Communism attempted to exterminate our culture. We survived, not without scars. The country's sense of loss is palpable, yet trauma has been swept under the carpet of economic growth and development. As quickly as Poland is recovering from its past, and as wonderful as it is to see our people spreading their once clipped wings, it is just as important to remember our roots. Many people have moved through and settled on this land, leaving imprints on our cuisine as they came and went. Despite the unthinkable end to Jewish culture in this area, Chicken soup (rosół) is a staple as are many fish and meat dishes which feature 'Jewish-style' variants. This is also true for more transitory ethnicities, such as the many Gypsies that came in and out of Poland throughout the centuries.

When travelling through modern Poland you still get a taste of these historical eras in our food – the famous *staropolski* style that you find in many a *karczma* (Polish inn) is the old-school traveller fare; the communist years are relived in the milk bars; whereas in the high-end contemporary city restaurant you will find the exciting taste of a modern Poland rediscovering itself.

My intention was not to write a typical, traditional Polish cookbook but to create something contemporary, a love letter to the country I left behind.

This book is my journey.

HISTORY

"POLSKĘ ŻEŚMY PRZEJEDLI I PRZEPILI"

"Too much eating and drinking cost us our Poland."

[Polish proverb]

This proverb beautifully describes the Polish love of food, drink and parties, which often led to us not being in the right frame of mind to defend our country from attack. Considering the number of enemies Poland had (both outside and within), it's understandable that we turned to these simple pleasures as a distraction

...out the
depart
Swedes,

ch and
ration,
d war
hanges
plain
s been
torian
und'.

now it,
en by
during
pagan

equivalent of a christening). Two strangers knocked on the door of his modest household, having been refused entry to the castle of the mean-spirited Prince Popielo. Although his feast was modest, Piast welcomed the strangers into his abode. The strangers turned out to have magical powers and made the food and drink grow and multiply creating a fantastical feast that the guests remembered for the rest of their lives. Once he'd grown up, the son of Piast, the lucky Siemiowit, drove out the Popiel prince, and formed the first Polish ruling dynasty called the Piasty Clan. This feast was the stuff of dreams and legends, yet it offers a perfect example of the Polish art of hospitality and entertaining. Everyone is welcome. Food and drink is to be shared amongst friends and strangers alike, snobbery or any kind of exclusion is unacceptable.

When talking to my grandmother about the ruling dynasties of Poland, I was surprised to learn that aside from the foremost Piasty clan, all Polish royalty had hailed from other countries. The Italian Queen Bona brought with her many vegetables (indeed the Polish word *włoszczyzna* which we use to describe vegetables, comes directly from our word for Italy); the famous Jagiellonian Dynasty started with the pagan Lithuanian King Jagiello and the Polish-Hungarian Queen Jadwiga, who left both Lithuanian and Hungarian traces on our cuisine and culture, Jan III Sobiecki brought Asian influences; and during the reign of the last Polish King, Poniatowski, French cuisine was *à la mode*. Poniatowski was also a lover of Catherine the Great of Russia, who it is said, placed him in his position of power. But it was the peasant cooking of Russia which had the greatest influence on our Polish cuisine, and that of course came from the common people rather than the royal court.

In addition, we cannot ignore the Polish Catholic bond with the Papal See. The church officials and urban elites looked to Italy for influences in every area of life, especially the kitchen. By the 18th Century, Polish aristocrats were writing about a golden age of Polish cookery, yet the dishes they wrote about were mostly from Tuscan or Milanese descent, adapted to suit Polish ingredients and tastes.

MEDIEVAL POLAND

The horse-bound, nomadic Tartars were a constant threat as their fierce hordes rampaged our lands on a regular basis, attacking the Slav settlers. Their culture has had an undeniable impact, reflected in dishes such as Steak Tartare – originally made from horsemeat minced under their saddles – and Tartar sauce – which is now commonplace European fare.

At the other end of the scale, some influences were positively welcomed into the country. During the Middle Ages, Poland was heavily influenced by Czech cuisine. While from the 14th Century onwards, Armenians were invited to settle on Polish land by an array of Polish Kings and brought with them many of their culinary traditions. It is more difficult to determine exactly where our Middle-Eastern influences came from but we do know that as well as the Armenian settlers, throughout the Middle Ages Arab traders came to our shores. Similarly, we don't know the exact date the Jewish settlers arrived, but it could be as early as the start of the formation of the Polish state. The increased persecution of people from surrounding lands also brought a steady influx of migrants over the centuries. By the 14th Century Polish King, Kazimierz Wielki (Casimir the Great), extended his royal protection to the Jews who were fleeing persecution in Silesia (then under rule of the Habsburgs).

We can taste the Middle East in the famous *gołąmbki* – cabbage leaves stuffed with rice and meat as well as the refreshing cucumber and yoghurt salad we eat during the summer. Bread and butter, soured milk, pickles, radishes, cumin, paprika and dill are popular in our culture, yet working out where these culinary influences came from is a bit like looking for a needle in a haystack. I suspect many popular Polish dishes originated in the homes of Armenian and Jewish immigrants and were adapted to include Polish ingredients and cooking methods. Cooking, like all oral traditions, was passed down from one family member or friend to another, as an everyday act of love and as a means of keeping these culinary heirlooms alive in the memories of each generation. And so, before literacy became widespread in Poland, these recipes only existed in the nations memory.

THE PARTITIONS

Between 1795 and 1914 Poland was wiped off the map of Europe and lived on only in the hearts of its inhabitants. During these partitions, Russian, Prussian and Austro-Hungarian cuisines officially ruled, depending on which part of Poland you were in. In the homes of Poles, food became a symbol of the old country, the last vestige of their national identity. The Polish cuisine endured although its land were fractionalised and it became a small, stubborn act of defiance in the face of national displacement. Ever since 1945, despite Poland's fragmented history and the maps being drawn and redrawn over and over again with ever-changing borders, the country has occupied more or less the same terrain as it did under its very first ruler – Mieszko I. Bitter irony, considering the amount of turmoil, destruction and human sacrifice expended on and over these lands in the last thousand years.

COMMUNIST POLAND

During the grey Communist years (1945–89), culture was viewed with suspicion and there was often nothing in the shops due to incompetency and mismanagement of resources. Yet again, Polish cuisine was kept alive mainly in peoples' homes and memories, as a symbol of their heritage and resilience. Despite the rations (it was not uncommon to find only vinegar on store shelves), or perhaps because of it, people paid the greatest care to maintaining their hospitable traditions in those days, sharing and swapping whatever food they managed to get hold of. Growing one's own fruit and vegetables, as well as foraging for food, became essential in this part of the world. The meagre food served outside of the home was bland and overcooked – the typical Communist Milk Bars stand as a living testament to this period in Poland's food history (ironically, many of which are now patronised by writers and artists, which means that the quality of the food served has greatly improved).

Many sources and records of culinary information were lost during this time of intolerance and political extremism. The burning of Poland's national archives in 1944 by the Nazis destroyed 75 per cent of the archived material of the aristocracy – a massive and unfortunate loss, since it was mostly the aristocracy that had the time and the inclination to indulge in the pastime of recording their recipes.

REGIONALITY

Geographically speaking, Poland sits at the crossroad between the East and the West of Europe. While this has often made it a battleground, it is the central point of all culinary influences. Spices from the Middle East came through Poland and were swapped for amber from the Baltic coast; from the West French and Italian influence proliferated. Due to Poland's rocky, divided history, some of its regions developed independently from others. Even though those old borders are no longer officially recognised, ethnographically speaking, they're still there, in our various traditions, culture, food and dialect.

Wind-swept and wild, coastal Pomerania crowns Poland, with Germanic Gdańsk being its most elaborate jewel. This stunning area, though rich in fish, has always had poor soil, so the cuisine is fish-heavy, with plenty of bread and potatoes as accompaniments. Kaszuby is the standout area for food and culture because the inhabitants are considered to be of a different ethnicity to the rest of Poland.

The equally attractive, yet polar opposite of Pomerania, is the Tatra mountains in the South, bordering on Slovakia. Although this is the most heavily explored Polish mountain range, it is also the most separatist. The mountain folk have preserved their own dialect and regional dishes, the most famous being the smoked sheep-milk's cheese *oscypek*, which has regional patterns engraved in its rind.

The magical, meandering waters of the Mazury Lake District have a special place in the collective heart of Poland. You would be hard-pressed to find a Pole who has not been here, either camping in the woods, sailing on the lakes or holidaying in a wooden hut on the water's edge. Here, the Poles eat fish from the lakes, with *surówka* (vegetable slaw), sausages on sticks roasted over a fire until they crackle and char on the outside, and various wild mushrooms freshly picked from nearby woods.

Małopolska and Wielkopolska (Little Poland and Greater Poland) were names ascribed to them during the Middle Ages, when the capital was still in Gniezno, before it moved to Kraków, then finally to Warsaw. The region around the old capital was therefore Greater Poland – Wielkopolska. It is a fertile region that is proud of its culinary heritage containing plenty of vegetables including its famous asparagus. Małopolska – Little Poland – on the other hand, has always been Lithuanian in its tastes.

Silesia (Śląsk) is an area rich in soil and resources, which not only borders with Germany and the Czech Republic, but is also very much a part of them. Bohemia and Greater Moravia were also historically in this region. The area is large and the cuisine varies from one town to the next, but universally it's known for its rabbits, dumplings, black pudding (blood sausages) and knysza (stuffed bread) and separatist spirit.

I am from the Mazowsze region, which is further east geographically and much further east in terms of its culture. It was in a Russian colony during the partitions, while in the Communist years it was still only three hours' drive from the USSR (now Bielosrus). Eastern Poland is where Oriental influences have always been felt more keenly, the original meaning of the word 'Oriental', means 'Middle-Eastern'. Paradoxically, as a result of this direct relationship with Russia and the East, this is also an area that is representative of Poland as a whole because its inhabitants have always worked hard to maintain the country's culinary traditions.

SEASONS

Winter is the time for bigos (Polish kimchi) and introspection. Seething winter punishes the earth and its inhabitants with a biting cold. When I was little there was so much snow in Poland that we used to make igloos; these days there is much less. Summer, on the other hand, is rich and golden. Filled with golden skin, light and whispering fields of wheat. Even in Eastern Europe this is the time for light foods, fun and dalliances, though I can't deny that there remains a certain Slavic melancholy during these carefree times, for we know only too well that everything must end and change according to the seasons. Even though everything is now available to buy in the shops, seasonality is still a prevailing factor in the way most people eat. Being in touch with nature and the earth is an integral part of our eating and cooking methods. Surviving harsh Polish winters throughout the ages led to the invention of pickling and preserving fish and vegetables. Whereas, during the long, hot summers there is an abundance of fresh, cooling food, such as our cold soups. Autumn is a time for our favourite national pastime of foraging for wild mushrooms, whereas in spring we look forward to the emergence of our first young vegetables. Although we love our food, we don't obsess over it, yet we do long for it; it's a truly romantic approach.

SPRING

After a harsh, frost-bitten winter, spring comes as a sigh of relief. Easter is an even bigger event than Christmas. Big, fluffy *baba* cakes are baked. Baskets full of dyed eggs, smoked sausage and other breakfast treats, along with little sugar lambs are blessed in church before being eaten. Such is the rhythm of life: fasting during times when the earth is barren which allows for the clearing away of the old and preparing for the new. The Easter feast is always a cold buffet of *zakąski*, as guests come and go all day long, with warm dishes being served at intervals. During spring the earth is pregnant with planted seeds and we anxiously await the arrival of our first vegetables. The custom goes that when you eat the first vegetable of the season you must grab the ear of the person that you are sharing it with, and whoever does it first will receive good luck for the year ahead. We still eat many things that are pickled and dried during spring, but we constantly move towards fresher tastes and lighter foods.

SUMMER

Summers are often stiflingly hot on these Eastern plains and due to the extended period of Communism and the political movement's preference for concrete high-rise accommodation for the masses, many Polish towns become suffocating, concrete jungles. Thus, hot days are usually spent in our allotments in the countryside, called the *działka*, or *dacha* (in Russian). Each piece of land, no matter how humble, is sacred to us as it's where we feel the most connected to the earth. In the summer, whenever possible, we eat outside. My childhood summer memories are always set within nature: family and friends congregating: eating cold beetroot soup in the

the welcome shade of fruit trees; my grandma sitting with a massive bowl between her chubby legs, shelling peas under an awning; adults playing cards and drinking vodka by the Vistula river while we children collected wild cherries for soup; older boys building a *szałas* tipi out of branches in the forest, potatoes and sausages sizzling in the fire at dusk; jumping into lakes and rivers, our sun-drenched skin flashing gold as we played... There were always big gatherings. Everyone brought something delicious and the earth provided the rest.

In the summer, Poles often travel to the enchanted waters of the Lake District, part of one of the imposing Tatra Mountains or the icing sugar soft beaches of the Baltic coast. Whose beaches are strewn with little bits of amber: tiny orange, brown and yellow transparent pebbles, as light as plastic. In the Middle Ages the merchants from Arabia would stop off in Poland on the way to Western Europe to swap their spices for this golden resin, which was believed to have healing qualities.

Summers here smell of pine – the hardy tree that has claimed these lands for millions of years – and tastes of freshly caught, fried fish washed down with cold beer. We have a long tradition of beer drinking and we are proud of the fact that one Polish King refused to go on a crusade to the Holy Land because he was not accustomed to drinking anything other than beer, so could not be parted from it.

AUTUMN

Early autumn is a period where the earth changes and we begin to prepare for the hard season to come. It's the time of leafy trees, glimmering shades of red, orange, yellow and brown under the final, warm summer rays. I have vivid memories of walking with my grandma Halinka in Łazienki Park, through a river of fallen leaves. At times the river reached my knees as I ran through it, collecting chocolate-coloured chestnuts and little green acorn heads that looked as if they were wearing berets similar to mine.

Then comes All Hallows Eve with its ocean of candles burning against the sad graves: an ethereal glow envelops the smoke-filled cemeteries where we spend Halloween; with those we have loved and lost. Walking through graveyards, we catch up with distant family members and elders reminisce about their younger days. This is a time of nostalgia, memories and melancholia (that we Eastern Europeans do so well).

During Autumn we begin our preparations, as the coming months will not be easy. Pickling is a typical way of preparing for the harshness of winter, where the frost and snow prevent anything from sprouting. Pickled mushrooms are very popular as are the dried varieties. At regular intervals, every household's nominated mushroom picker will go into the nearest forest and methodically re-visit each of their secret spots. Even in her advanced old age, my grandma Ziuta, used to spot a beautiful

'Cossack' (a fitting nickname for a tanned and proud prince of mushrooms) from afar, hidden in the undergrowth. Then there are all the other foraged pickles: gherkins, beetroot, cabbage, red peppers and pumpkins, – all of which will keep us fed and our larders stocked throughout the coming season.

WINTER

Winter has a severe yet glistening beauty. Bare black branches cast ink onto creamy skies, frosty lace covers the naked earth and when the snow comes it forms a welcome duvet upon the land.

We start preparing for Christmas in mid-December. I grew up in the times of Communism, it was during these hard years that a large part of our preparation was spent trying to source food. This seemingly simple part of the process actually took a great deal of time and effort. It was about families and friends working collectively to ensure they gathered all they needed for the upcoming festivities, it was that communal sense of pulling ourselves together against all odds that made Christmas day even more special. You'd need a carp for Christmas Eve, a goose or turkey for Christmas day, and that's not even taking into account all the other ingredients that you need for the 12–13 non-meat dishes (one for each of the apostles, some also count Jesus) that we eat on Christmas Eve and the meaty dishes for the day after. The tradition was to keep the carp alive in the bathtub until the very last moment, so that it was as fresh as possible when eaten. This meant that the carp took priority over anyone else in the household; no one could have a bath until the carp was finally out of the tub and on the slab.

What fills the Christmas table depends on where you are, but for my family it's always been: Russian salad, *ryba po Grecku* (pollock in an aromatic sauce), various types of herrings, either fish in aspic or fish marinated in vodka, fresh bread and butter. The first warm course was usually *barszcz z uszkami* (borscht with little ears). An hour or so later, there would be a fried fish meal such as carp. After another short break *kapusta z grzybami* (sauerkraut stew with wild mushrooms and beans) would emerge, piping hot from the kitchen. Finally, dried fruit *kompot* (stewed dried fruits) would accompany the assortment of cakes, in order to help you digest. Traditionally, you would be drinking a lighter version of the fruit *kompot* throughout the evening, along with vodka. In my family we tend to prefer champagne as an accompaniment to this meal, interspersed with an occasional shot of vodka. The cold dishes remain on the table until it's time for the sweets. Essentially, the whole evening is about trying as many dishes as possible – folkloric wisdom decrees that the more things you try during this feast the more varied and complete the following year will be.

INGREDIENTS

In today's technological world Poland may not be that far away from the West, yet in terms of ingredients we are still quite far apart. We have many of the same fruit and vegetables, but there are different variants, which can make all the difference taste-wise to a dish. A good example is the yellow beans (also called wax beans) – they look a lot like green beans, yet have an entirely different taste and texture. They are very common in Poland – yet strangely difficult to find elsewhere. Luckily, with the Internet at our fingertips, we can get hold of almost anything.

There are many Polish shops dotted around the world and there are often Polish sections in the World Food isles of many supermarkets. Many Turkish and Italian specialist ingredients would work well as a replacements to their Polish counterparts.

I only buy meat when I know its origins, and I suggest you find your own organic butcher. However, if you do pick up your meat from supermarkets, only buy the best you can afford, preferably organic. If an animal had a good life, it will reward you with the benefits of its meat.

BREAKFAST AND BREAD

Breakfast is my favourite meal of the day and it's the main reason I get out of bed in the morning, especially when I'm at my family home in Poland, as my mother prepares it every morning. Whenever my brother and I return home, it's treated as a special occasion by my parents, judging by the breakfasts feasts they prepare. It's an ancient, unwritten law of Polish hospitality that makes us treat the arrival of guests as an opportunity for a celebration – as well as our natural inclination to enjoy the smaller things in life.

The Polish breakfast is a brunch-esque affair, it can be sweet or savoury and often both. The range of recipes that are considered to be typical Polish breakfast fare are vast and varied, depending on which part of Poland you find yourself in. While my late grandma, Babcia Ziuta, always started the day with sweet kasza (semolina porridge), my Babcia Halinka (my other grandma), always preferred open sandwiches (*kanapki*) – which are fresh slices of rye bread with cold cuts of meat on a base of crunchy salad leaves and onion-sprinkled tomatoes, homemade gherkins and marinated red peppers. Whereas most working Polish men will not be satisfied until they get their share of protein in the morning; therefore scrambled eggs will be eaten in their homes for breakfast, with onion, tomatoes, chanterelles or crispy fried pieces of dried Polish sausage. It's also completely normal to find Polish breakfast tables filled with many different things; breads, cold cuts of meats, salads, cheeses and sweet cakes. The only rule that applies across the board for Polish breakfasts is that there must be one warm dish, be it eggs, frankfurters, breakfast soup, omelette or *kaszanka* (black pudding/blood sausage made with toasted buckwheat groats).

One thing is clear: breakfast is a vital meal in this part of the world and plays a large part in our festive seasons such as Christmas, Easter and other national celebrations. For when we breakfast we 'break' our 'fast', and due to the Polish cultural emphasis on fasting it makes morning feasting all the more relevant and necessary. For instance, our Christmas breakfast is always a great feast because we have fasted all of Christmas Eve.

We also fast throughout the Lent period and when Easter Sunday finally comes around, we take our eggs and sausages to the Church to be blessed by the priest. We dye our eggs with beetroot juice or onion skins and decorate them with traditional folkloric designs. We then place them all on a lacy, white napkin in a basket, along with some bread, salt and pepper, and anything else that the family feels will make their basket stand out from the other lovingly prepared family Easter baskets (decorations such as sugar lambs, fluffy chicks, catkins from the willow tree and springtime flowers such as daffodils are often used). After their baskets are blessed in Church, the family returns home and eat their boiled eggs with sincere thanks, it is a breakfast rich in food and national symbolism.

Each mouthful of these soft, spongy and sweet pumpkin *zacierki* dumplings never fails to transport me back to my childhood. My mother made this soup for me throughout my childhood, when pumpkins were in season, as her mother had done for her as a child. This soup typifies a mother's love for her child. **{Serves 4–5}**

SWEET PUMPKIN BREAKFAST SOUP WITH ZACIERKI DUMPLINGS

150–200 g (5–7 oz/scant 1¼–1⅔ cups) plain (all-purpose) flour
1 egg, beaten
1 small pumpkin, around 1 kg (2 lb 3 oz)
700 ml (1¼ pints/3 cups) full-fat milk
freshly grated nutmeg
1 tablespoon caster (superfine) sugar
large pinch of salt

First make the dumplings. Tip the flour into a large bowl and mix in the egg and a tablespoon of water until the mixture forms a dough ball, add another tablespoon of water if the dough isn't coming together. Knead the dough ball for a few minutes; it's ready when it is no longer sticky and falls away easily from your hand, add more flour if it still feels too sticky.

Make the *zacierki* by ripping little bits of the dough ball off and forming them, between two fingers, into very small oblong shapes, like a cardamom pod or orzo pasta. Don't take too much time on the formation of them, because it could take hours to create perfectly uniformed pieces. These dumplings should be quick and easy to make (as a guide 2 seconds on each one is more than enough). It's fine if they are all different shapes and sizes.

Peel and deseed the pumpkin, then chop into 2.5 cm (1 in) chunks. Place in a pan, cover with water (so that they are covered with not much excess water on top) and cook over a medium heat for about 25 minutes, or until completely soft. The pumpkin should be falling apart when you stir it.

In a separate pan, bring the milk up to a gentle simmer. Add the *zacierki* to the milk and cook for 5 minutes. Grate some nutmeg into the milk while the *zacierki* are cooking. The *zacierki* are ready when they have a squidgy and soft texture.

Combine with the pumpkin mixture, adding sugar and a little bit of salt to taste. Then simmer them together for a couple of minutes, until the pumpkin has completely fallen apart and has infused the soup with a rich orange colour.

{Time: 30 minutes}

Once you've tried these refried pancakes stuffed full of sweet, white cheese, you'll never look back. It is best to use the Polish cheese *twaróg* (available from any good Polish shop), but you can also use ricotta or another fresh white cheese instead. If you have any of this cheese leftover at the end, you can serve it as a cold snack, with jam or honey, either on its own or on some crusty, freshly buttered bread. **{Serves 4}**

NALEŚNIKI WITH SWEET CINNAMON CHEESE

Make the pancake batter: tip the flour into a bowl, add the egg and whisk in the milk until you have a smooth batter which has the consistency of double (heavy) cream. Add a pinch of salt and the vanilla extract (if using) and whisk again.

Melt a little of the butter in a small frying pan (skillet). Cook the pancakes one at a time ensuring they are reasonably thin, as you will be wrapping them around a filling. Add 4 tablespoons of batter and swirl to coat the base of the pan. Cook for a couple of minutes, then flip over and cook the other side. Repeat with the remaining batter, adding more butter to the pan as needed until you have made eight pancakes.

Use a fork to mash the *twaróg* with the yoghurt, sugar and cinnamon. Add the egg yolk and continue mashing. Finally, stir in the raisins.

Put a couple of heaped teaspoons of filling in a thick line on one-third of a pancake and roll it up like a burrito: fold the two ends in first, then roll around the filling quite tightly to make a roll that's 5–8 cm (2–3 in) wide and 12–15 cm (5–6 in) long. Repeat with the remaining pancakes and filling.

Heat the remaining butter in a frying pan over a medium heat and fry each pancake until crispy on each side.

Serve immediately with a drizzle of single cream.

{Time: 25 minutes}

FOR THE PANCAKES

250 g (9 oz/2 cups) plain (all-purpose) flour
1 egg
300 ml (10 fl oz/1¼ cups) milk
pinch of salt
1 teaspoon vanilla extract (optional)
100 g (3½ oz/7 tablespoons) unsalted butter

FOR THE FILLING

300 g (10½ oz) *twaróg* (or ricotta)
2 tablespoons Greek yoghurt
1 tablespoon caster (superfine) sugar
1 teaspoon ground cinnamon
1 egg yolk
1 tablespoon raisins

single (light) cream, to serve

A simple, rustic dish made with Poland's favourite fruit, the apple. This cinnamon-apple bake was popular during Communist times – when the queues for food were miles long – as the only ingredient that the Polish people never ran out of were apples. This is perhaps why the Polish apple is looked on with such a sense of national pride.

Any tart apple, such as a cooking apple, works well in this recipe. The best rice to use is soft and sticky pudding rice, although risotto rice is a good substitute. The idea is to have thick layers of juicy, sweet apples and thin layers of rice in between. **{Serves 4–6}**

CINNAMON-APPLE BAKE

6–8 cooking apples, peeled, cored and chopped
150–200 g (5–7 oz/1–1¼ cups) raisins
200 g (7 oz/1 cup) soft light brown sugar, plus extra for sprinkling
1 teaspoon ground cinnamon
¼ teaspoon freshly grated nutmeg (optional)
400–500 g (14–18 oz/2¼–scant 3 cups) cooked pudding rice
250 ml (8½ fl oz/1 cup) single (light) cream

Preheat the oven to 180°C (350°F/gas 4).

Put the chopped apples in a bowl with the raisins, sugar, cinnamon and nutmeg (if using) and mix to combine.

Layer a third of the apples in the bottom of a baking dish, followed by a thin layer of cooked rice; another layer of apples and another of rice, finishing off with a final layer of apples.

Bake in the oven for 30 minutes, then pour the cream over the top and sprinkle with more sugar. Return to the oven for a further 20 minutes. Serve piping hot.

{Time: 1 hour}

This fruity, 'sponge cake' omelette – *omlet biszkoptowy* – is not the kind of savoury omelette you would usually find in the West and it's far tastier than your average sponge cake. For the berries, use whichever ones are in season or locally available. If you have any spare egg whites from baking, then add an extra one (or even two) to the recipe for even more fluffiness. For every extra egg white add an additional half tablespoon of flour. **{Serves 2}**

FLUFFY OMELETTE WITH STEWED BERRIES

150 g (5 oz) mixed berries
50 g (1¾ oz/3½ tablespoons) caster (superfine) sugar
4 eggs, separated
4 tablespoons plain (all-purpose) flour
1 tablespoon unsalted butter
crème fraîche and honey, to serve

First stew the berries: put them in a pan with the sugar and a tablespoon of water. Cover and cook over a low heat until they have burst and released their juices – this should take about 10 minutes.

In a bowl, whisk the egg whites until stiff peaks form, then start adding the yolks, one by one, followed by the flour.

Heat half of the butter in a small frying pan (skillet) and once it's hot pour in half of the mixture to make one omelette. (If you have two frying pans, you can make both omelettes at the same time.)

Fry over a medium heat for about 2–3 minutes on each side. Some people grill (broil) the other side but if the omelettes are quite small then you shouldn't have a problem flipping them over; just shake the pan and make sure that the omelette is moving before quickly flipping to soft side down.

Top with the stewed berries, a dollop of crème fraîche and a drizzle of honey.

{Time: 20 minutes}

For savoury breakfast lovers, this egg and onion combination is a dream. Only caramelised onion can bring this kind of depth and flavour to such a simple dish. This is why it's both mine and my father's favourite scrambled egg recipe. Freshly buttered bread or bagels are an absolute necessity. **{Serves 2}**

CARAMELISED ONION SCRAMBLED EGGS

1 tablespoon salted butter
1 onion, finely chopped
5 eggs
splash of milk
pinch of sweet paprika
salt and white pepper, to taste

Melt the butter in a large frying pan (skillet) and add the chopped onion. Cover the pan and cook over the lowest possible heat for about 15 minutes.

For the final 7–8 minutes, remove the lid and stir occasionally, seasoning with salt and white pepper near the end of the frying time. The edges should crisp up slightly, but not char, as this will make your scrambled eggs taste bitter.

Meanwhile, whisk the eggs with a splash of milk, a little bit of salt and a pinch of paprika.

Finally, pour the eggs over the onion and fry over a low heat, stirring almost continuously for the final 3–4 minutes that it takes to get the scrambled eggs to the consistency you prefer.

{Time: 25 minutes}

Gzik hails from the rich and fertile Wielkopolska region. If you cannot get hold of Polish *twaróg* cheese, then you can replace it with a creamy cottage cheese (in which case you should omit the yoghurt).
{Serves 4}

RYE BREAD WITH CRUNCHY GZIK

250 g (9 oz) *twaróg* (or cottage cheese)
4–6 tablespoons Greek yoghurt or soured cream
bunch of radishes, finely chopped,
bunch of chives, finely chopped
salt and white pepper, to taste
8 slices of buttered rye bread, to serve

Mash the *twaróg* with a fork and add the yoghurt or soured cream. Continue mashing until the consistency becomes soft and silky. Use as much yoghurt or soured cream as you need to achieve your desired consistency.

Add the finely chopped radishes and chives (reserving a few to garnish), season well with salt and pepper and mix together.

Spread onto buttered rye bread and garnish each slice with some reserved chopped chives.

{Time: 5 minutes}

This is the breakfast of our farmer ancestors. *Kasza manna* is the name we give to semolina and milk porridge, as well as the grain itself. This is a nutritious breakfast harking back to the olden days, where grains were our main source of carbohydrates. It was also my grandma Ziuta's breakfast of choice. **{Serves 4}**

KASZA MANNA: SEMOLINA AND HONEY PORRIDGE WITH RASPBERRIES

200 g (7 oz/generous 1 cup) semolina
4 tablespoons cold water
400 ml (14 fl oz/1¾ cups) milk
pinch of salt
150 g (5 oz/1¼ cups) raspberries
1 teaspoon caster (superfine) sugar
2–3 tablespoons good-quality honey

Before you cook semolina you need to mix the grains with a tiny bit of cold water to form a smooth paste – if you were to put the grains straight into hot milk you would get clumpy *kasza*.

Pour the milk into a pan with a pinch of salt and place over a medium heat.

In a separate pan, heat the raspberries and sugar, covered, over a low heat, until the raspberries begin to fall apart and release all of their lovely juices.

Once the milk is close to boiling, start slowly stirring in the semolina paste with a wooden spoon. Turn the heat down and simmer for about 3–4 minutes. Add 2 tablespoons of the honey, taste and add more if you want it sweeter.

Serve the porridge in a bowl with the syrupy raspberries spooned on top.

This porridge is also delicious when it has set, just chill it in the fridge and serve it once it has cooled.

{Time: 15 minutes}

{*Rogaliki* with Lilac Jam}

The aroma of these yeasty *rogaliki* lilac-filled buns baking in the oven never fails to bring reassurance to my soul. When I was growing up, there was a lilac bush growing near my grandma Halinka's home, a pre-war building on a hill overlooking Warsaw. In the springtime, the lilac's heady smell would follow me as I walked towards her home.

Some people like to make their *rogaliki* very neat, but I'm convinced that they aren't as tasty; I like the filling to spill out while they're cooking so that the sticky filling sweetens the dough, so I always add just that little bit too much. If your *rogaliki* don't look very neat, then don't worry, they'll taste all the better for it! **{Makes 20}**

ROGALIKI WITH LILAC JAM {see pages 38–39}

25 g (scant 1 oz) fresh yeast
100 ml (3½ fl oz/scant ½ cup) tepid milk
1 tablespoon vanilla sugar or 1 tablespoon sugar and ½ teaspoon vanilla extract
250 g (9 oz/2 cups) plain (all-purpose) flour
2–3 tablespoons soured cream
125 g (4½ oz/1 stick plus 1 tablespoon) butter
pinch of salt
lilac jam (see page 252) or any other jam for filling

Combine the yeast with the tepid milk and vanilla sugar (or sugar and vanilla extract) in a large bowl and mix well.

Add all the other ingredients (apart from the filling) and mix until it comes together in a ball. Knead for a few minutes until the dough comes cleanly away from your hand.

Put this ball of dough into a large pan or container filled with warm water. When it rises to the top of the bowl, it's ready.

Preheat the oven to 180°C (350°F/gas 4). Take the ball of dough out of the water and place on a floured work surface. Knead it again, dusting with flour regularly to stop it from sticking, then roll the dough out as thinly as you possibly can.

Use a knife to cut the dough into triangle shapes, about 8–10 cm (3–4 in) at their base and 12-14 cm (5–5½ in) tall. Place a teaspoon of jam on the shortest side of each triangle and roll the edge over the top of the filling. Keep rolling the dough until you get to the end and then bend the ends slightly to create a *rogalik* (crescent) shape.

Place the *rogaliki* on a baking tray lined with baking paper (parchment paper) and bake in the oven for 45 minutes. Allow to cool for a few minutes before eating – as the jam will be piping hot!

{Time: 45 minutes}

This is my grandma Halinka's recipe, although I have replaced the apples with plums. *Racuchy* is super easy to make, especially if you have four hands working together. When we make them at home, one of us beats the egg whites and prepares the plums, while the other makes the dough. This makes a lot of *racuchy* – enough for five people with some leftover. It's one of those dishes that you may as well make a large amount of, as you can eat them the next day and you'll always eat more than you think. **{Serves 4–6}**

PLUM RACUCHY WITH SOURED CREAM

300 g (10½ oz/2½ cups) plain (all-purpose) flour
1 tablespoon vanilla sugar
pinch of salt
1 teaspoon baking powder
2 eggs, separated, plus 2 egg whites
250 ml (8 fl oz/1 cup) milk
1 tablespoon rapeseed oil, plus extra for frying
1–2 tablespoons natural yoghurt
500 g (1 lb 2 oz) plums, stoned and thinly sliced
icing (confectioners') sugar, to serve

Combine the flour, vanilla sugar, salt and baking powder in a bowl. Stir in the egg yolks and then pour in the milk and mix with a wooden spoon for about 5 minutes. Add the oil and yoghurt and stir again – the mixture should have as few lumps as possible.

In a separate bowl, beat the egg whites until they form stiff peaks. Fold the egg whites into the mixture and then add the plums.

Heat a thin layer of oil in a frying pan (skillet) over a high heat and then reduce to medium heat when you begin to fry the mixture. Use a tablespoon to spoon the mixture into the hot oil – one spoonful makes one *racuch*. Fry them, in batches of four or five, for about 3 minutes on each side. Drain on kitchen paper (paper towel) and repeat until the mixture is all used up, adding more oil to the pan for each batch. Serve hot and dusted with icing sugar.

{Time: 30 minutes}

"O GOOD BREAD, WHEN IT IS GIVEN TO GUESTS WITH SALT AND GOOD WILL."

{Wespazjan Kochowski}

In the olden days, bread with salt was given to guests as they arrived at your home as a mark of respect and goodwill. It's a symbolic gesture that is still repeated to this day in many different guises. In the cellars of Warsaw Old Town, where the famous basilisk was once said to have roamed, which now houses many traditional Polish restaurants, bread with pork dripping and gherkins is presented to guests on arrival, to munch on while perusing the menu. The welcoming of guests with bread has morphed in many households into a bringing out of *zakąski* (see page 174–175) upon guests arrival, or alternately, open sandwiches *kanapki*. A symbolic version of this custom is the sharing of holy bread before a Christmas meal, when everyone shares their wishes and hopes for one another in the coming year.

Bakeries in Poland are always full of different types of bread: white country loaves, rye, rye with prunes, spelt, multigrain and that's just the sourdoughs. Then there are the yeast products too – buns stuffed with bilberries or sweet cinnamon cheese and all sorts of other ready-to-eat delights. By the 14th Century in Kraków (the capital at the time) there were nine different varieties of bread being baked daily and our love affair with bread has only increased since – going to a bakery to buy your daily bread is still an everyday occurrence for Polish people.

"Do kraju gdzie kruszynkę chleba
Podnoszą z ziemi przez uszanowanie dla darów Nieba…
Tęskno mi Panie."
"Oh Lord how I miss
The country where even a crumble of bread
Is picked up from the ground out of respect for the gifts from God."
{Cyprian Norwid Moja Piosenka}

Wheat is perfectly suited to the landscape of this country and has become an intrinsic part of our cuisine. When Christianity was brought into our lands around the year 1000 A.D. bread became a symbol of Christ in communion. Even to this day, bread is still sacred to us, when I was little my grandma Halinka taught me to kiss a piece of bread if it ever fell on the floor, as a mark of respect for all food which feeds and nourishes us. We still hate throwing away stale bread, as superstition tells us it will bring bad luck and hunger. With this reverent attitude to bread bubbling away in our collective subconsciouses, we do various things with stale bread rather than throwing it away, such as making breadcrumbs or adding it to pâtés and soups.

Baking your own own bread is a pleasant, therapeutic, grounding experience that feels good for the soul. It's going back to basics in the most homely, loving way you possibly can.

Sourdough bread is not only extremely tasty, but it's also very good for you. The secret of its goodness lies in the fermentation process; fermented foods may be all the rage nowadays, yet they have been a cornerstone of the Polish cuisine for generations, as a means of preserving foods through the long, cold winters.

If you are happy to put in a little bit of effort every day over the course of a week, do consider making your own sourdough starter. In my experience, rye flour makes the strongest, most resilient starter. If you keep the starter in the fridge it will get better and stronger over time and will improve the more you use it. **{Makes 1 large jar, approx 300 ml (10 fl oz)}**

SOURDOUGH STARTER

150 g (5 oz/scant 1½ cup) organic wholegrain rye flour
150 ml (5 fl oz/⅔ cup) water

Simply mix the flour and water together in a large glass jar and cover with a tea towel (dish towel). (I use an elastic band to keep the cover in place.)

Leave it for three or four days at room temperature, stirring once a day. By day three or four bubbles should have formed on the top of the starter; at this point you need to feed it. If you don't have bubbles, then it hasn't worked so start the process again or if a mould has developed start again. It won't smell lovely at this point, but neither should it smell revolting.

If all the signs are good, it's feeding time! Discard half of the starter and replace it with the same amount of fresh flour and water. Allow this to stand once more at room temperature for two more days, then repeat the feeding process. After a further two days the starter is ready to use in your bread. Use however much you need, then replenish the starter with fresh flour and water.

Twenty-four hours after feeding it, store the jar in the fridge. Remember to use the starter at least once a week, or take some out and feed it.

{Time: 10 minutes, plus resting time}

This recipe is dedicated to my uncle Wojtek, who is my mother's youngest brother, my godfather and a master breadmaker. He got me hooked on bread making and now I hope I can pass this love onto you – in fact, it was he who gave me my first sourdough starter.

For this recipe I have used three parts rye flour to one part plain flour, just to add a little softness to the rye. The pumpkin seed oil I have used in this recipe is available in organic food stores and even some supermarkets. However, if you can't find it, any other oil will work fine and this bread will still be delicious. **{Makes 1 x 900 g (2 lb) loaf}**

PUMPKINS AND OTHERS SIMILAR ARE NATIVE AMÉRICONS CULTIVATED THERE.

SOURDOUGH RYE WITH PUMPKIN SEEDS

300 g (10½ oz/2½ cups) rye flour
100 g (3½ oz/generous ¾ cup) plain (all-purpose) flour
2 teaspoons salt
3 tablespoons wheatgerm
2–3 tablespoons pumpkin seeds
1 tablespoon oats
2 tablespoons sourdough starter (opposite page)
250 ml (8½ fl oz/1 cup) tepid water
1 tablespoon pumpkin seed oil

Grease a 900g (2 lb) loaf tin with butter and dust with flour.

Place both flours into a large bowl with the salt, wheatgerm, pumpkin seeds and oats. Stir well to combine.

Mix the starter with the tepid water. You can do this either by pouring the water into the jar you keep the starter in and shaking them together really well or just mix them using a spoon. Add this mixture to the dry ingredients in the bowl and continue mixing in one direction, until you get a dough the consistency of peanut butter, then add the oil. Knead the dough in the bowl for about 5 minutes to get some air into it.

Place the dough into the prepared loaf tin, cover with a tea towel and leave in a warm place to rise, such as near a radiator, for 10 hours.

Preheat the oven to 180°C (350°F/gas 4). Bake the loaf in the oven for 1 hour, or until dark brown and it should sound hollow when tapped. This sourdough bread will keep for about 5 days.

{Time: 1 hour 15 minutes, plus rising time}

Spelt has been cultivated for over 7,000 thousand years and continues to bring us a wealth of nutritional goodness as well as its gorgeous, nutty taste. If you don't have rapeseed oil you can substitute it with any mild-tasting oil. **{Makes 1 x 900 g (2 lb) loaf}**

SPELT SOURDOUGH WITH CRISPY ONIONS

2 tablespoons rapeseed oil
1 onion, finely chopped
300 g (10½ oz/2½ cups) wholegrain spelt flour
100 g (3½ oz/generous ¾ cup) rye flour
2 teaspoons salt
3 tablespoons wheatgerm
1 tablespoon oats
2 tablespoons sourdough starter (see page 46)
250 ml (8 fl oz/1 cup) tepid water

Heat the oil and fry the onion over a low-medium heat until they are golden and slightly crispy at the edges, stirring occasionally. This should take about 20 minutes.

Meanwhile, mix both flours, salt, wheatgerm and oats together in a large bowl.

Mix the starter with the tepid water, ideally shaking it in a jar. Add this to the dry ingredients in the bowl and continue mixing in one direction, until you get a dough the consistency of peanut butter. Add the crispy fried onions and knead the dough in a bowl for about 5 minutes to get some air into it.

Place the dough into a greased and floured 900 g (2 lb) loaf tin, all in one go if you can manage, cover with a tea towel (dish towel) and leave in a warm place to rise, such as near a radiator, for 10 hours.

Preheat the oven to 180°C (350°F/gas 4). Bake the loaf in the oven for 1 hour, or until it sounds hollow when tapped. This bread will keep for about 5 days.

{Time: 1 hour 30 minutes, plus rising time}

Somewhere in the depths of the Podlasie region, there was once a baker who made dark rye bread wrapped in horseradish leaves. This sounds like a fairytale, but when I read about this baker I decided I had to make a similar bread, with the addition of caraway seeds – also common around these parts and much loved in neighbouring Lithuania. It was the best bread I had ever made. I don't know if it was down to the horseradish leaves, but they certainly made it look interesting, the sort of bread you imagine woodland fairies might feast on. **{Makes 1 large round shape loaf}**

DARK CARAWAY RYE IN HORSERADISH LEAVES

300 g (10½ oz/2½ cups) rye flour
1 teaspoon salt
2 tablespoons wheatgerm
1 tablespoon caraway seeds
1 tablespoon sourdough starter (page 46)
150 ml (5 fl oz/⅔ cup) tepid water
1 tablespoon rapeseed oil
2–3 horseradish leaves (including 1 large one), optional

Combine the flour, salt, wheatgerm and caraway seeds in a large bowl.

Mix the starter with the tepid water, ideally shaking it in a jar, until it is completely dissolved. Add this to the dry ingredients in the bowl and continue mixing in one direction, until you get a dough the consistency of peanut butter.

Add the oil and knead the dough with floury hands on a floured surface, bending the edges in and pressing down with your body weight, for about 7–8 minutes, until you have a smooth ball of dough.

Place the dough ball on the largest horseradish leaf and wrap with the remaining, smaller leaves. Leave the dough to rise in a warm place, near a radiator, for 9–10 hours.

Preheat the oven to 180°C (350°F/gas 4). Place the loaf, still wrapped in the leaves, on a baking tray and bake in the oven for 1 hour, or until it sounds hollow when the tapped. This rye bread will keep for about 5 days.

{Time: 1 hour 15 minutes, plus rising time}

When it comes to creativity I've found that some of the best results are born from mistakes. Cooking is no different, mistakes are always welcome in my kitchen. This bread accidentally came to fruition during this book's photoshoot in Poland. I woke up at 7 a.m. and started to make *rogaliki* dough. My mother pointed out that I'd made the wrong dough, but once I had drunk some coffee and felt more awake, I transformed it into this twist (which is a traditional folk design). I had never intended to have a brioche-style bread in this book, but fate clearly wanted it to be involved so who was I to stop it? **{Serves 20}**

FLUFFY WHITE TWIST WITH RAISINS

125 ml (4 fl oz/½ cup) milk
20 g (¾ oz) fresh yeast
50 g (1¾ oz/¼ cup) caster (superfine) sugar
250 g (9 oz/2 cups) plain (all-purpose) flour
2 egg yolks
30 g (1 oz/2 tablespoons) softened unsalted butter
½ teaspoon vanilla extract
75–100 g (2½–3½ oz/ ½–⅔ cup) raisins
egg white, to glaze

First warm the milk in a pan and stir the fresh yeast into it, along with a tablespoon of sugar and all the flour. Keep mixing until the mixture is smooth and free of lumps. Cover with pan with a tea towel (dish towel) and leave in a warm place to double in size, approximately 30 minutes–1 hour.

Blend the egg yolks with the remaining sugar until well combined and then add to the *rozczyn* (yeasty mixture) in the pan along with the butter and vanilla extract and blend well.

Knead for 7–12 minutes on a floured surface (depending on your muscle). Add the raisins as you knead. The more air you get into the dough the better. Cover the dough once again and leave for about 30 minutes, or until doubled in size. Preheat the oven to 180°C (350°F/gas 4).

Tip out onto a floured surface and knead some more, adding more flour to make it more manageable – you'll need a good few handfuls. Divide the dough into two and roll each piece into a long sausage shape, about 30 cm (12 in) long. Twist the two together and then seal the ends.

Transfer the twist to a baking tray lined with baking paper (parchment paper) and brush all over with the egg white to glaze. Bake in the oven for 40 minutes, or until golden. This bread is best eaten within the first 2 days of making it.

{Time: 1 hour, plus rising and proving time}

Sesame seeds always remind me of my homeland. We used to eat them as caramelised sesame snaps, inside fudge and on top of pretzels and bread buns.

These buns are simple to make and are a fantastic accompaniment to both *zakąski* and soup. However, it is worth bearing in mind when you make bread with yeast, it always tastes better on the day of baking, when it's still slightly warm and fresh; as it will be considerably drier the following day. I have chosen to use instant dried yeast for these buns as you don't have to mix it with milk or water first. **{ Makes 9–10 buns}**

EASY SESAME SPELT BUNS

250 g (9 oz/2 cups) wholewheat spelt flour
250 g (9 oz/2 cups) plain (all-purpose) flour
75 g (2½ oz/½ cup) sesame seeds
½ teaspoon salt
14 g (½ oz) instant dried yeast (2 sachets)
1 egg, beaten
200 ml (7 fl oz/scant 1 cup) tepid milk

Preheat the oven to 180°C (350°F/gas 4) for 5 minutes and then turn it off.

Sift the two flours into a bowl to aerate them, adding the spelt wholegrain bits left in the sieve after sifting. Keeping some sesame seeds aside for the topping, add all the rest of dry ingredients to the flour and mix well.

Reserving a little of the yolk to glaze the buns before baking, add the rest of the egg to the bowl. Use your hands to bring the ingredients together into a soft dough, adding the milk a little at a time (increase the milk if needed). Knead the dough in the bowl for about 5 minutes, or until the dough comes away from your hand. Cover the bowl with a clean, damp tea towel (dish towel) and place it in the warmed oven to rise for about 1½ hours.

When the dough has increased in size it's time to start kneading. Turn the dough out onto a floured surface and pull and stretch a portion of the dough away from you and fold or punch it back into the middle. Turn the dough slightly and repeat this process until the dough is beautifully smooth. If you knead aggressively then 10 minutes should suffice. Meanwhile, preheat the oven to 180°C (350°F/gas 4) and line a baking tray with lightly greased baking paper (parchment paper).

Divide the dough into 9–10 pieces and roll each one into a ball – about half the size of a tennis ball. Flatten them slightly and place them on the tray and add them straight into the hot oven. After 30 minutes the buns should look golden brown and sound hollow when tapped. Brush the tops with the reserved egg yolk and sprinkle over the reserved sesame seeds. Return to the oven for a further 10 minutes to finish baking.

{Time: 1 hour, plus rising time}

BUTTERS

One of the things that age has taught me is that the best things in life are usually the most simple! These butters are no exception – just butter and a couple of other carefully chosen ingredients spread on homemade bread – that's the kind of medicine that nourishes your soul. They keep in the fridge for 10 days (but in my house they never last more than a week). Once you have one of these butters in your fridge, you will be putting it on everything.

Anchovy butter has such a fantastically strong, umami flavour that it only needs to be added on fresh bread or a jacket potato for maximum enjoyment. The most important thing to remember here is to avoid salted butter. If you only have salted butter in the fridge then avoid making anchovy butter as this will give you a salt-induced heart attack!

{Makes 275 g (10 oz)}

ANCHOVY BUTTER

75 g (2½ oz) canned anchovies in oil
200 g (7 oz/scant 1 cup) unsalted butter, softened

Drain the anchovies from the oil and add to a food processor or blender along with the butter. Whizz until completely blended, stopping to scrape down the sides of the bowl occasionally. Alternatively, you can blend the anchovies and butter using a pestle and mortar.

Transfer to a little serving dish and chill in the fridge for at least 30 minutes before serving.

{Time: 2 minutes, plus chilling time}

"BYŁA SOBIE BABA JAGA
MIAŁA CHATKĘ Z MASŁA
A W TEJ CHATCE SAME DZIWY...

*"There was an old witch, Baba Yaga
She lived in a hut made of butter
And in it, so many wondrous things..."*

{Ancient Polish Lullaby}

This pink butter is a pretty addition to any table. You can vary the amount of beetroot you use, depending on how pink you want your butter to be. If you would like to go for a light, pastel pink then half a beetroot will be sufficient. Garlic loves salt so I like to crush them together first to really fuse these two flavours together. **{Makes 275 g (10 oz)}**

PINK BEETROOT BUTTER

1 garlic clove
large pinch of sea salt
1 small beetroot (beet), cooked and roughly chopped
200 g (7 oz/scant 1 cup) salted butter, softened

Use the back of a heavy knife to crush the garlic with the salt until combined.

Add to a food processor or blender with the chopped beetroot and butter. Whizz until completely blended, stopping to scrape down the sides of the bowl occasionally. Alternatively, you can pound the beetroot, garlic and butter using a pestle and mortar.

Transfer to a small serving bowl and chill in the fridge for at least 30 minutes before serving.

{Time: 2 minutes, plus chilling time}

The forest brings us many gifts, yet we've grown unaccustomed to accepting them. Chanterelles are the only wild mushrooms that are enjoyed around the world, but I truly hope that this will change and that many more wild mushrooms will become widely available. **{Makes 275 g (10 oz)}**

CHANTERELLE BUTTER

200 g (7 oz/scant 1 cup) salted butter, softened
1 garlic clove, crushed
large handful of chanterelles
pinch of salt

Heat a small knob of the butter in a frying pan (skillet) over a low-medium heat. Add the garlic and chanterelles and fry for about 5 minutes, stirring occasionally. Add a pinch of salt to season.

Tip the contents of the pan into a food processor or blender and add the remaining butter. Whizz until smooth, stopping to scrape down the sides of the bowl occasionally.

Transfer to a serving bowl and chill in the fridge for 30 minutes before serving.

{Time: 8 minutes, plus chilling time}

SOUPS

There are hundreds upon hundreds of Polish soups. However, due to Poland's complicated national history, some of them aren't exclusively Polish and many of the recipes have multi-national roots. It would take an entire book to delve into the history of Polish soups and to do them all justice. Instead, this chapter includes a selection of my Polish favourites which are both seasonal and regional.

A typical Polish main meal would be served between 3–4 p.m. and would invariably be a soup followed by a main course – no other starter can replace soup in the heart or stomach of a Pole. Consequently, in any Polish household you enter, there is always some sort of soup on the go, either still cooking, piping hot or chilling in the fridge waiting to be eaten.

There are, of course, specific types of soup for different seasons and regions, indeed some regional soups are so specific that you will not find them anywhere else in Poland, like the beautiful fisherman's soup that I ate every day on a recent visit to the seaside resort of Sopot. I found this gem, made from various unused boat-fresh bits of fish in a tomato broth with marjoram and other herbs and spices, in an unpretentious hut on the beach next to where the fishermen sold their daily catch. The hut was just 100 metres from the hotel and the soup cost less than a pound, so eating this fish soup on the beach became my daily ritual. Even more local, is a soup called *Rakowiecka* that a friend of my parents proudly displayed on his restaurant menu, named after a political jail, where most of the *Solidarność* movement and other anti-communist activists resided at one point or another. It is a very light, vegetable broth (as you would expect from prison food). We like to remember our past here – however unpleasant – and it's worth taking a moment to applaud the bravery of those that ate this soup until their dying day, because they refused to bow to a regime that forbade them from speaking freely. Historically, there are even certain soups that would be given to a suitor when he came to propose to the family (as that's how proposals took place in those days). *Czarna Polewka* (duck blood soup or black broth) would be served as a rejection and pea soup was served as both a 'yes' and a 'no', depending on how the pig's tails were arranged on the soup.

Borscht could have it's own chapter dedicated to it, as there are so many varieties in Poland! We commonly eat clear Warsaw-style borscht with *pierogi* or *uszka*, but the only thing our clear borscht has in common with the rich Ukrainian version is that beetroot is a key ingredient. Then there are the Polish fruit soups. We eat these when a particular fruit is locally available, usually in the summer months. Eating a fruit soup in the winter would remove the all-important association between the soup and the time of year. You could cheat a little bit with this seasonal fruit soup rule, as I believe a sunny spring day, with local rhubarb and frozen strawberries is just about acceptable. The one exception to this rule is a soup made from dried fruit, which is really more of a compote and smells of Christmas.

{All the quantities given in this chapter are for a large batches of soups – about 8–10 servings per pot and all therefore need approximately 2 litres (4 pints/8½ cups) of water (more if they are cooked for a long time). Remember that, despite what some people say, soup often tastes better the day after it's made.}

The name *chłodnik* comes from the word *chłód* (cold), which perfectly exemplifies that the purpose of this popular soup is to cool you down on a hot summer's day.

Chłodnik is traditionally made from beetroot with the addition of yoghurt, crunchy vegetables and, most importantly, it's served straight from the fridge. In Mazowsze, we mostly eat it with hard-boiled eggs, yet for this Lithuanian version I've added some cold smoked chicken breast instead. As this soup originates from Lithuania, I have honoured its roots, but feel free to swap the chicken breast for hard-boiled eggs. **{Serves 8–10}**

COOL LITHUANIAN CHŁODNIK FOR HOT DAYS

- 1 kg (2 lb 3 oz) young beetroot (beet), with stalks
- 2 litres (4 pints/8½ cups) water
- large bunch of radishes, diced
- 1 large cucumber, peeled and diced
- bunch of dill, finely chopped
- bunch of chives, finely chopped, plus extra to garnish
- 250 ml (8 fl oz/1 cup) soured cream
- 250 ml (8 fl oz/1 cup) natural yoghurt
- juice of 1 lemon
- caster (superfine) sugar, to taste
- salt and white pepper, to taste
- sliced smoked chicken breast, to serve

Finely chop the beetroot, including the stalks. Add to a large pan with the water and place over a high heat. As soon as it comes to a simmer reduce the heat and cook for about 40 minutes, until the beetroot is tender when pierced with a knife. Remove from the heat and allow to cool for about 1–1½ hours.

When cool, add the radishes, cucumber, dill and chives to the pan. In a separate bowl, mix together the soured cream, yoghurt and lemon juice and then stir into the pan. Season to taste with sugar, salt and pepper. (I usually add the same amount of salt and sugar and just a bit of pepper but it is important that you taste and adjust to your liking.) Mix everything thoroughly. Transfer to a serving bowl and chill in the fridge for at least 1 hour before serving.

To serve, pour the chilled soup into each bowl, then top with sliced smoked chicken and some reserved chives. You can also use hard-boiled eggs, in place of the smoked chicken to top the soup.

{Time: 1 hour, plus cooling time}

Wild cherries (*wiśnie*) are sour rather than sweet and are not as popular outside Eastern European countries. In Poland you can buy them everywhere at the right time of year, while in other parts of the world they may need to be foraged or sourced online.

I make this as a sweet soup, although back in the old days it was common to eat it with new potatoes topped with dill. If you would like to try this rather sophisticated, savoury pairing, just leave out the cinnamon and cloves and reduce the amount of sugar by half. You should also leave out the *ptysie* balls (similar to choux pastry but light and fluffy) and only serve it with soured cream. **{Serves 8–10}**

WILD CHERRY SUMMER SOUP

FOR THE PTYSIE BALLS

40 g (1½ oz/3 tablespoons) salted butter
80 ml (3 fl oz/⅓ cup) water
100 g (3½ oz/generous ¾ cup) plain (all-purpose) flour
large pinch of bicarbonate of soda (baking soda)
2 eggs

FOR THE SOUP

500 g (1 lb 2 oz) wild cherries, pitted (if unavailable, use normal cherries but reduce sugar to 25 g (scant 1 oz/2 tablespoons)
2 litres (4 pints/8½ cups) water
½ teaspoon whole cloves
½ teaspoon ground cinnamon
50 g (1¾ oz/scant ¼ cup) raw cane sugar
2 tablespoons potato flour
1 tablespoon water
soured cream, to serve

First make the *ptysie* balls. Preheat the oven to 200°C (400°F/gas 6) and line a baking tray with baking paper (parchment paper).

Put the butter and water in a pan and heat gently. As soon as the butter has melted start slowly sifting in the flour (pre-mixed with the bicarbonate of soda), stirring all the time until you have a smooth paste. Allow the dough to cool to room temperature, then add the eggs and beat well until the dough comes away from the sides of the pan to form a ball, you can add a little bit more flour at this point if the dough is too sticky. Tear off tiny little pieces of the dough and roll into roughly 40–50 balls. Place on the baking tray and bake in the oven for 30 minutes, or until golden. Remove from the oven and allow to cool to room temperature.

Put the cherries, water, cloves, cinnamon and sugar into a large pan and place over a high heat and bring to the boil, then reduce the heat to medium and simmer for 15 minutes, until the cherries are soft.

Mix the potato flour with the tablespoon of water until you have a smooth paste. Stir this into the soup to thicken it and then simmer for a further 5 minutes.

This soup is always served at room temperature so leave it to cool for at least 30 minutes before serving. Serve it with a dollop of soured cream and a few *ptysie* balls floating on the top.

{Time: 1 hour 15 minutes, plus cooling time}

This is a simple soup, based on a very old, country recipe that I once received from a lady who sold me a bag of sorrel at our local market in Poland, who told me it was her grandma's recipe. I have substituted some of the sorrel for nettles in this recipe, but if you can't source nettles, then either replace the nettles completely with sorrel or use some peppery watercress instead. **{Serves 8–10}**

FORAGERS' SOUP WITH SORREL AND YOUNG NETTLES

200 g (7 oz) sorrel and young nettles
50 g (2 oz/4 tablespoons) unsalted butter
2 litres (4 pints/8½ cups) water
3 tablespoons plain (all-purpose) flour
150 ml (5 fl oz/⅔ cup) Greek yoghurt
salt and white pepper, to taste
hard-boiled eggs, to serve

First remove the nettle leaves from their stalks (wearing gloves to protect your hands) and thoroughly wash the sorrel and nettle leaves.

Melt the butter in a large frying pan (skillet) and add the sorrel and nettle leaves. Fry for a few minutes over a medium heat until wilted. Set aside to cool for about 20 minutes and then transfer to a food processor or a blender and whizz to a purée.

Transfer the purée to a large pan and add the water. Bring to a boil, then reduce the heat and simmer for 20 minutes, stirring occasionally. Near the end of the cooking time, season the soup with salt and pepper and sprinkle in the flour, stirring all the time. Increase the heat and boil for 5 minutes, allowing the flour to thicken the soup.

In a bowl, add a tablespoon of the hot soup to the yoghurt, to prevent it from curdling.

Swirl a tablespoon of yoghurt into the soup and then place two hard-boiled egg halves into each bowl. You can turn this soup into a more substantial meal by serving potatoes on the side.

{Time: 50 minutes}

Beetroot soup – borscht or *barszcz* as we call it in Poland – is known in many different guises. This dramatic looking, crimson soup is the richest variety of borscht there is and can be served as a meal due to its thick, stew-like consistency. The traditional recipe uses soured beetroot juice but I've simplified the recipe by just adding some lemon juice and soured cream. **{Serves 5}**

RICH UKRAINIAN BORSCHT WITH BEEF AND BUTTER BEANS

First prepare the meaty base for the soup. Place the steak in a large pan with the pimento berries and the bay leaf. Pour over the water and bring to the boil, then reduce to simmer for about 20 minutes. Remove the steak from the pan, chop into bite-sized pieces and set aside.

Now add the carrots, parsnips, celery, leek and potatoes into the same pan and gently boil in water over a medium heat for about 35 minutes, until the vegetables are soft.

Meanwhile, in a separate pan, boil the beetroot in the water until they are tender (again about 35 minutes), then peel and either dice into chunks or cut into strips (as you prefer). Add this mixture to the vegetables along with the chopped tomatoes and butter beans. Season with salt, pepper and sugar. If the soup is not red enough, you can always add some more beetroot juice.

When the potatoes are completely soft add the lemon juice, chopped parsley and reserved steak pieces. Taste and adjust the seasoning before serving with a dollop of soured cream and some fresh parsley to garnish.

{Time: 1 hour 15 minutes}

150 g (5 oz) large rump (top round) steak
1 teaspoon pimento berries
1 bay leaf
2 litres (4 pints/8½ cups) water
2 carrots, grated
2 parsnips, grated
2 celery stalks, finely chopped
1 leek, finely chopped
3 potatoes, peeled and diced
4 beetroot (beet), diced or sliced
1 x 400 g (14 oz) can chopped tomatoes
2 x 400 g (14 oz) cans butter (lima) beans
250 ml (8 fl oz/1 cup) beetroot (beet) juice (optional)
2 tablespoons lemon juice
handful of freshly chopped parsley, plus extra to garnish
salt, pepper and sugar, to taste
soured cream, to serve
fresh parsley, to garnish

The oldest recipe for Christmas Eve borscht comes from the 16th Century and it is very similar to this recipe except it calls for soured beetroot juice. This is not a soup you can eat on it's own, as it's more of a drink, that you use to wash down other, solid foods, and can even be served in a cup. It is most commonly eaten with *uszka* (see page 169) but it would also work well with other dumplings, such as crispy *pierogi* (see page 167).

If you cannot get hold of dried boletus mushrooms, you can use any other dried mushrooms. **{Serves 8–10}**

CLEAR VEGETARIAN BORSCHT

- 10–15 dried mushrooms, preferably boletus (if unavailable, use any dried mushrooms)
- 3 litres (5¾ pints/12 cups) water
- 4–5 beetroots (beet), peeled
- 1 carrot
- 1 parsnip
- ½ celeriac (celery root)
- 1 celery stalk with leaves
- 1–2 bay leaves
- 5–6 allspice berries
- 5–6 black peppercorns
- 2 tablespoons lemon juice
- 1 tablespoon dried marjoram
- 1 teaspoon caster (superfine) sugar
- salt and white pepper, to taste

Wash the mushrooms. Place them in a bowl, covered with boiling water and leave to soak for 1 hour. Transfer to a pan with the liquid, add about 1 litre (2¼ pints/4 cups) water, bring to the boil then reduce the heat to a simmer and cook for about 2 hours.

Meanwhile place the beetroots, carrot, parsnip, celeriac, celery, bay leaves, allspice berries and peppercorns into a separate pan and add 2 litres (3½ pints/8 cups) water. Bring to a simmer and cook for 1 hour.

Strain both broths through a sieve into a clean pan (you can keep the cooked vegetables, chop them into small dice and combine with mayonnaise to make the Slavic salad, see page 200). Add the lemon juice, marjoram and sugar and season well with salt and pepper.

Return to the heat and simmer for about 15 minutes. Taste before serving, adding more sugar, salt or pepper to taste.

{Time: 2 hour 15 minutes, plus soaking time}

"TEN KRAJ PACHNIE JAK DYMIĄCA WAZA GORĄCEGO BARSZCZU Z GRZYBAMI..."

"This country smells of a steaming tureen of hot borscht with wild mushrooms."
{Stanisław Brzozowski}

After many years of practice and experimentation my mother has perfected the art of making Polish tomato soup. Her recipe has medicinal, soothing qualities – good for both the body and soul. The base is made in exactly the same way as a typical Polish chicken soup *rosół*. The only tweak I have made to her recipe is to substitute the chicken for turkey, as I prefer its flavour and its greater nutritional value. **{Serves 8–10}**

SOOTHING TURKEY AND TOMATO SOUP WITH RICE

1 turkey thigh
1 parsnip, peeled
3 carrots, peeled
2 celery stalks
1 bay leaf
5–7 pimento berries
2 litres (4 pints/8½ cups) water
250 ml (8 fl oz/1 cup) tomato passata
1 tablespoon tomato purée (paste)
1 teaspoon caster (superfine) sugar
150 ml (5 fl oz/⅔ cup) single (light) cream
salt and black and white pepper, to taste
cooked white rice, to serve

Cook the turkey thigh with the parsnip, carrots and celery stalks with the bay leaf and pimento berries in a pan filled with the measured water, over a medium heat for at least 1 hour.

Remove the vegetables and turkey thigh from the pan with a slotted spoon, discarding the parsnip and celery stalks. Chop the carrot into slices and remove the meat from the turkey thigh.

Add the passata and tomato purée to the soup and continue to simmer for another 10 minutes. Add the sugar and season with salt and both peppers.

In a medium bowl, blend the cream with a tablespoon of the hot soup to prevent it from curdling before adding into the pan. Then, add the sliced carrots and flaked turkey meat and taste the soup to see if it needs further seasoning.

Serve with cooked white rice in bowls.

{Time: 1 hour 20 minutes}

The perfect time to make this soup is in early spring, when fresh, local rhubarb is still available and it's just about warm enough to sit outside and soak up a few of those shy, early spring rays. This is another Polish soup that's eaten either slightly chilled or at room temperature. This creamy strawberry and rhubarb soup is just the kind of sweet, light soup that you would finish a meal with. **{Serves 8–10}**

CREAMY STRAWBERRY AND RHUBARB SOUP

- 2 large stalks of rhubarb, peeled and roughly chopped
- 2 litres (4 pints/8½ cups) water
- 1 teaspoon cloves (about 7 or 8)
- ½ vanilla pod (bean)
- 1 kg (2 lb 4 oz/7 cups) strawberries
- 4 tablespoons caster (superfine) sugar
- 300 ml (10 fl oz/1¼ cups) single (light) cream
- 50 g (1¾ oz) cooked conchigliette pasta per person (or any other small pasta shapes)

Place the rhubarb into a large pan with the water, cloves and vanilla pod and bring to a boil, then reduce the heat to medium and simmer for 20 minutes, or until the rhubarb is soft.

Meanwhile, mash the strawberries and sugar together in a bowl with a potato masher. Add to the pan, reduce the heat to low and cook together for a further 20 minutes.

Let the soup cool (cover it and put it outside if you can) for at least 30 minutes before adding the cream.

Place the cooked pasta in the bottom of each bowl and pour over the soup.

{Time: 50 minutes, plus cooling time}

This soup is full of character, thanks to the unique, ancient flavour of wild mushrooms. Some people prefer to eat this mushroom soup as an alternative to borscht on Christmas Eve: its lightness makes it a perfect fasting soup. **{Serves 8–10}**

CLEAR WILD MUSHROOM SOUP WITH CRISPY PASTA

100 g (3½ oz) dried wild mushrooms, porcini if available
2 litres (4 pints/8½ cups) boiling water
1 carrot
1 parsnip
1 onion
2 celery sticks
2 tablespoons salted butter
400 g–500 g (14–18 oz) cooked penne
salt and white pepper, to taste

Wash the mushrooms and place in a bowl. Cover with boiling water and drain. Then add 500 ml (18 fl oz/2 cups) of boiling water the second time and leave the mushrooms to soak for a good couple of hours as you'll be adding this brown, flavoursome water into the soup.

To make the vegetable stock, put the carrot, parsnip, onion and celery in a large pan and cover with 1½ litres (2½ pints/6¼ cups) water. Add plenty of salt and bring to a boil then simmer for about 50 minutes. Remove the vegetables from the pan with a slotted spoon and discard.

Strain the mushroom liquid into the vegetable stock, reserving the mushrooms. Season to taste and bring the stock up to a simmer. Chop the mushrooms and add to the pan and continue to cook for a further 30 minutes.

Meanwhile, melt the butter in a frying pan (skillet) over a high heat. Add the cooked and drained penne pasta and fry for about 7–8 minutes, stirring occasionally, until crispy.

Serve together in the same bowl.

{Time: 1 hour 30 minutes, plus soaking time}

Krupnik is akin to a really posh vegetable soup, much loved in Poland and perfect for the colder months. Like many things in life, *krupnik* improves over time – for me it tastes best on the third day of cooking. Like most vegetable soups in Poland, the stock is made from meat, a little trick that has caught out many an unsuspecting vegetarian! **{Serves 8–10}**

WINTERY KRUPNIK WITH PEARL BARLEY AND FRESH HERBS

Place the chicken thigh in a large pan with the carrots, celeriac, parsnip, leek and bay leaves. Add enough water to cover and bring to a boil and then turn right down to a simmer and cook over a low heat for 20 minutes.

Add the allspice berries, peppercorns, potatoes and pearl barley to the pan and simmer for 30–40 minutes, until both the potatoes and pearl barley are cooked.

Meanwhile, fry the bacon lardons until crispy while the soup is simmering.

Add the sugar to the soup and season with salt and both peppers. Add the fresh and dried herbs and continue to cook over a very low heat for a further 5–10 minutes.

Finally, add the bacon bits to the pan and serve.

{Time: 1 hour 10 minutes}

1 large chicken thigh
4 carrots, grated
1 celeriac (celery root), peeled and grated
1 parsnip, grated
1 leek, chopped
2 bay leaves
6 allspice berries
6 whole black peppercorns
4 potatoes, peeled and cubed
200 g (7 oz/scant 1 cup) pearl barley
handful of bacon lardons
1 teaspoon caster (superfine) sugar
2 tablespoons chopped fresh dill
2 tablespoons chopped fresh parsley
1 tablespoon chopped fresh lovage (or ½ tablespoon dried lovage)
salt and black and white pepper, to taste

This is a typical Easter soup; we eat it for Easter Sunday breakfast (more of a brunch really). I remember once staying in a B&B run by nuns in the Polish mountains and they served this every morning – which was a great way to start a 12-hour hike!

This is a soup for when you're feeling brave and experimental, it is an unusual recipe because you make soured rye (*żur*) for the base. You can buy this in most Polish shops although it is easy to make. Ideally you would use Polish white sausage for this, but I've found good Cumberland sausages work very well as a replacement. **{Serves 8-10}**

SOURED RYE ŻUREK IN A TRADITIONAL BREAD BOWL

FOR THE SOURED RYE

4 tablespoons rye flour
400 ml (14 fl oz/1¾ cups) warm water
1 garlic clove, crushed slightly with the side of a knife

FOR THE SOUP

1 onion
1 carrot
1 parsnip
1 celeriac (celery root)
2 sausages
1 bay leaf
1 boletus mushroom (optional)
2 litres (4 pints/8½ cups) water
4 tablespoons brine from a jar of gherkins (optional)
2 rashers (slices) bacon, cut into strips
1 tablespoon dried marjoram
100 ml (3½ fl oz/scant ½ cup) single (light) cream
plenty of salt and white pepper
large bread rolls, to use as bowls

First prepare your soured rye. Mix together the rye flour, warm water and crushed garlic in a glass jar until thoroughly combined. Cover the top of the jar with a cloth and leave in a warm place in your kitchen for 5 days to sour. Give it a stir once every day.

To make the soup, you can char the onion on a stove to give it an additional smoky flavour. Or you can simply add all the vegetables into a large pan with 1½ sausages, bay leaf, boletus mushroom (if using), marjoram and (charred or uncharred) onion. Add the water and bring to a boil and then simmer over a medium heat for 1 hour.

Strain the soup into a clean pan, reserving the sausages (discard the vegetables). Add the soured rye, brine juice (if using) and return the soup to the stove. Simmer gently for about 5–10 minutes, stirring often, and checking for seasoning.

Meanwhile, roughly chop the reserved ½ sausage. Fry the chopped bacon and sausages together in a frying pan (skillet) for about 5 minutes, until crisp.

Add a tablespoon of the hot soup to the cream to prevent it from curdling, then add the cream to the soup. Taste the soup and check again for seasoning.

The traditional way to eat this soup is in a large, round, crusty roll that has been hollowed out, topped with fried bacon and lardons. Make sure you don't hollow the rolls out too much – as it's utterly delicious to get mouthfuls of seeped-through bread.

{Time: 1 hour 20 minutes, plus fermentation time}

This soup was not a Christmas tradition in my family, as it was in so many other Polish households, therefore it gained an almost mythical status in my young imagination. It became a symbol of something slightly familiar yet just out of reach and deeply exotic.

In the traditional Polish recipe cow's milk is used, but as this is an almond soup and I think almond milk (now so commonly available) gives it the ideal modern twist. **{Serves 8–10}**

CHRISTMAS SWEET ALMOND SOUP

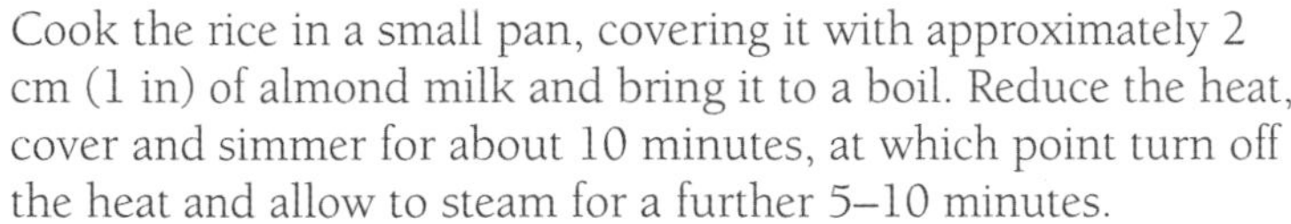

100 g (3½ oz/½ cup) white rice
1.5 litres (3 pints/6⅓ cups) almond milk
125 g (4 oz/1⅓ cups) ground almonds
4 tablespoons soft brown sugar
½ teaspoon ground cinnamon
2 tablespoons orange blossom water
50 g (1¾ oz/½ cup) flaked (slivered) almonds
large pinch of salt

Cook the rice in a small pan, covering it with approximately 2 cm (1 in) of almond milk and bring it to a boil. Reduce the heat, cover and simmer for about 10 minutes, at which point turn off the heat and allow to steam for a further 5–10 minutes.

Meanwhile, toast the ground almonds in a large, dry frying pan for about 7–8 minutes, stirring constantly. When you start to smell their distinctive nutty fragrance, add the sugar and 4 tablespoons of almond milk and keep stirring until it forms a paste-like consistency.

Pour the paste into the pan with the cooked rice. Cover with the remaining almond milk, add the cinnamon, pinch of salt and orange blossom water and bring to a simmer.

Allow this to bubble away for 5–10 minutes over a very low heat while you toast the flaked almonds. When they turn golden, add them into the soup, reserving a tablespoon to garnish.

{Time: 30 minutes}

MEAT

"TOUTE LA POLOGNE EST LE PLUS BEAU PAYS DE CHASSE QUE JE JAMAIS VU."

"The entire country of Poland is the most beautiful hunting ground that I've ever seen."

{Jean Francois de Regnard, 1655–1709}

Perceptions of Poland as a meat-loving country are not unfounded. As a Catholic country our culinary culture is based on fasting and feasting, during times of fast we eat fish, while the feasting is marked by the presence of a multitude of meats. As with many other Catholic countries, pork is very popular, and we have many well-loved cured meats and dried sausages such as *kabanosy* and *myśliwska*. When looking at Poland's history there is no denying the influence that hunting has had on the Polish cuisine. All types of game are still revered in the kitchen, even though we do not hunt like we used to.

"MILEJ PATRZEĆ NA DZIEWKĘ KTORA JEDZIE PIĘKNIE NA KONIU ZE SAJDAKIEM NIŻ KIEDY SIĘ OCIĄGNIE CIASNYM INDERAKIEM."

"A girl who rides a horse with grace, bow and arrow in hand, is more pleasing to the eye than when she's in a tight dress bound."

{Marcin Bielski, 16th Century}

I love the sentiment behind this quote, the appreciation of a woman's hunting skills and her somewhat wild nature, talent and freedom of spirit. For the 16th Century it seems remarkably progressive, although within the context of the Polish-Lithuanian Commonwealth perhaps unsurprising, as it was hailed as the most religiously tolerant and progressive land in Europe at the time with a multi-ethnic population of approximately eleven million.

We are a nation of game lovers and having read many historical Polish cookbooks I have found not only many recipes for game itself, but also recipes which make other meats taste more gamey! If you don't eat meat on a daily basis, then I would suggest going to a good butcher once or twice a week and trying out some local game and unusual cuts on the days that you do decide to treat yourself.

The preferred meat of choice depends on Polish regionality: the separatist seaside Kaszuby area is known for its geese; Śląsk, an area with German and Austrian influences, specialises on cooking rabbit in many different ways; whereas in Poznań, they love their duck. It is only in the Kresy area – on the border of Belarus and Ukraine – that meat becomes less popular, as it comes second place to mushrooms, blinis and *kaszas*, though veal and lamb are considered to be a rare treat. When looking at the country as a whole, pork seems to be the most popular of all the meats on offer due to its versatility. It's found in many dishes, though sometimes only in small quantities, simply as a means to enhance flavour.

Cold lands have "forests"
Tropical lands have "jungles" → Wilderness

Two ancient woodlands once existed in the region that this recipe originates from – The White Wilderness and The Green Wilderness. Within these two forests lived the Kurpie people. The *puszcze* (jungle) provided these forest dwellers with all they needed to survive. As the Kurpians were so cut off from the rest of the Poland they developed their own customs, traditions, dialect, dress and – most importantly – recipes, which are based on foods that were gifted to them by the Wilderness. **{Serves 2–3}**

CRISPY DUCK WITH APPLE AND WALNUT SAUCE

- 1 large duck breast, about 500 g (1 lb 2 oz)
- ½ teaspoon marjoram
- 2 tablespoons walnuts
- 1 apple, peeled, cored and cut into very small dice
- 1 tablespoon lemon juice
- freshly grated nutmeg
- 1 shallot, finely chopped
- salt and white pepper, to taste

Score the skin of the duck with a sharp knife. Mix the marjoram with some salt and white pepper and rub this mix all over the skin of the duck. Place in the fridge to marinate for at least 45 minutes, preferably 2 hours if you have time.

Lightly crush the walnuts then toast them in a dry frying pan (skillet) for a couple of minutes, until they start to turn golden. Remove from the pan.

Preheat the oven to 180°C (350°F/Gas 4). Place the diced apple on a baking tray and squeeze over the lemon juice. Grate over some nutmeg and place in the oven while it heats up.

Place the duck breast skin side down in a cold, non-stick frying pan over a medium-high heat for about 3 minutes, until the skin turns golden. Turn the duck over and cook the other side for just 30 seconds. Remove from the pan and place the duck on top of the apples in the baking tray. Return to the oven for 10 minutes.

Remove from the oven and rest the meat, covered with foil, for 10 minutes while you finish making the sauce. In the same pan as you cooked the duck, using its fat and juices, fry the shallot for a few minutes. Add the roasted apple pieces and toasted walnuts. Season with salt and white pepper to taste and cook for a further 2 minutes.

Crisp the skin of the duck by putting it under a preheated grill for 2 minutes, then slice the rested duck breast into thick slices and pour the sauce over it and serve immediately. This dish goes well with Beetroot purée (see page 142) and mashed potato.

{Time: 40 minutes, plus marinating and resting time}

Venison steaks prepared in this elegant, antiquated manner are deeply evocative of old Poland. Those refined olden days at the beginning of the last century: an airy, white *dworek* (small Polish manor house), a table decorated with wild flowers, white fabrics billowing in the warm breeze…

This rather romantic dish is incredibly simple to prepare. In the colder months, I would suggest serving it with a side of simple mashed potato and Beetroot purée (see page 142), in the warmer months: local asparagus and new potatoes with dill would be an excellent accompaniment. **{Serves 2}**

VENISON STEAK WITH PRUNE SAUCE

35 g (1¼ oz/2½ tablespoons) unsalted butter
2 x 150 g (5 oz) venison steaks
2 x 150 g (5 oz) pitted prunes, quartered
250 ml (8 fl oz/1 cup) red wine
25 g (1 oz/2 tablespoons) plain (all-purpose) flour
salt and white pepper
ground black pepper

Melt a knob of the butter in frying pan (skillet) over a medium-high heat. Season the steaks with salt and black pepper. Add the venison steaks and fry for about 3 minutes on each side. Remove from the pan, cover and leave to rest for 10–12 minutes while you make the sauce.

Add the remaining butter to the same pan that you cooked the venison in: you want to make use of the venison juices which will give your sauce extra depth of flavour. Add the prunes and fry, stirring, for a couple of minutes. Add the wine and bring to the boil, then immediately reduce the heat to a gentle simmer. Add the flour while stirring to thicken the sauce. Cook for about 7–8 minutes, until the sauce has reduced. Season the sauce with salt and white pepper, then pour over the venison and serve with mashed potato.

{Time: 25 minutes, plus resting time}

Every Polish household has their own version of a 'little pigeons' dish. While some are stuffed with meat, others are vegetarian; where some use *kasza* in the filling, others use rice; although most recipes call for the use of white cabbage, I have seen some that use red cabbage!

As Poland has had a large Armenian community within its midst since the 14th Century, I believe this much-loved national dish probably has its true roots in the Middle East. This is my own version, that gives a nod to the Middle Eastern origins of this dish. One cabbage makes about ten 'little pigeons'. The parcels need to be tightly packed so as not to fall apart during cooking. **{Makes 10}**

LAMB AND RICE STUFFED 'LITTLE PIGEONS' IN A CINNAMON-TOMATO BROTH

1 leafy cabbage
rapeseed oil, for frying
1 onion, finely chopped
500 g (1 lb 2 oz) minced (ground) lamb
1 teaspoon ground cinnamon
250 g (9 oz/scant 1½ cups) cooked short-grain white rice
1 litre (1¾ pints/4¼ cups) vegetable stock
3 tablespoons tomato purée (paste)
1 bay leaf
4 whole black peppercorns
salt and white pepper, to taste

Preheat the oven to 150°C (300°F/gas 2).

Wash the cabbage thoroughly while you bring a large pan of water to a boil. Blanch the cabbage for a couple of minutes, then remove from the pan and separate the larger leaves (the smaller leaves can't be used to wrap the parcels up with), cutting away the hard stalk. Drain the leaves on kitchen paper while you begin to make the filling.

Add a little rapeseed oil to a pan and fry the chopped onion over a medium heat for about 2 minutes, until softened. Add the lamb and continue to cook for about 4–5 minutes, until the meat has browned all over, breaking meat up with a wooden spoon as you do so. Halfway through cooking the lamb, add half the cinnamon to the meat and season with salt and white pepper. Remove from the heat, combine with the cooked rice and allow to cool slightly.

Meanwhile, combine the vegetable stock with the tomato purée, the bay leaf, peppercorns, remaining cinnamon and some salt and pepper.

Take one of the cabbage leaves and put a couple of tablespoons of filling in the middle. Fold it over lengthways, fold in both short edges and roll over to make a neat parcel. Place vertically inside an overproof dish, then continue with the remaining cabbage leaves and filling – you should have enough to make 10 parcels.

When the entire dish is packed full, pour over the stock mixture. Any smaller cabbage leaves that could not be rolled can go on top, to act as a lid. Bake in the oven for 1 hour.

{Time: 1 hour 30 minutes}

Although goulash originated in Hungary, in Poland it is more of a stew than a soup. We leave out the potatoes in the goulash and instead eat them with our *placek* potato cake – which is typical Polish mountain fare.

Goulash is the kind of stew that tastes even better the day after cooking, so I suggest making more than you need. If you don't feel like making the *placek* again, then serve it with toasted buckwheat groats and a gherkin on the side. **{Serves 1–2}**

OUTLAW'S PLACEK WITH GOULASH

First make the goulash. Heat the oil in a large, heavy-based pan over a low-medium heat and fry the onion, celery and carrot for about 3 minutes, stirring occasionally. Stir in the paprika and quickly add the beef to the pan. Fry for about 2 minutes, then add the peppers and pour over the wine.

Dissolve the beef stock cube in hot water, pour it into the pan and allow to simmer, covered, over a low heat for 40–45 minutes. The better quality the meat the less time it needs to cook.

While it's simmering make each *placek*. Finely grate the potato, onion and half of the carrot so that they turn to mush. Squeeze out any excess liquid from the mixture with your hands and place in a bowl. Add the flour and egg and season with plenty of salt and pepper.

Heat the oil in a large, ovenproof frying pan (skillet) over a medium-high heat. When the pan is smoking hot, tip in all of your *placek* mixture. Fry for about 10 minutes. Preheat your grill (broiler) and then grill (broil) the top of the *placek* for a few minutes. (This *placek* is about five times larger than a normal one and it's difficult to turn it at this stage.) As soon as the top has some colour and solidity to its form you can flip it over carefully and continue frying for a further 2–3 minutes.

Serve the goulash inside the *placek*: to do this you slide the *placek* onto one half of a large plate and then spoon the goulash on top, covering one half of the *placek* and spilling the rest onto the plate. Add a dollop of soured cream to the goulash and then fold the *placek* over the goulash.

{Time: 1 hour}

FOR THE GOULASH

1 tablespoon rapeseed oil
½ onion, chopped
½ celery stalk, chopped
½ carrot, diced
1 tablespoon smoked paprika
150 g (5 oz) sirloin beef (porterhouse steak), cubed
½ red (bell) pepper, diced
½ orange, yellow or green (bell) pepper, diced
250 ml (8 fl oz/1 cup) red wine
1 beef stock cube
50 ml (1¾ fl oz/scant ¼ cup) hot water
1 tablespoon ground flaxseeds or 1 tablespoon plain (all-purpose) flour and 25 g (1 oz/2 tablespoons) unsalted butter

FOR EACH PLACEK

1 large potato, peeled
½ onion
½ large carrot or 1 small carrot
1 tablespoon plain (all purpose) flour
1 egg, beaten
1 tablespoon rapeseed oil
salt and white pepper, to taste

soured cream, to serve

This is a typical, north, central cold semi-forest
European

In the west of Poland lie the vast lands of Silesia, which have had a rather complicated history due to the number of different rulers it's had. After the rebellion of its Polish speaking populace, a large part of Silesia was eventually handed over to Poland, although parts of it still lie in the Czech Republic (old Bohemia) and share many aspects of its culture and cuisine. The cooking of these lands is, understandably, influenced by the Czech Republic, Slovakia and Southern Germany. Even though the cuisine varies from one part of Silesia to another, all Silesians love rabbits, both to breed and to eat. **{Serves 4}**

BOHEMIAN CARAWAY ROASTED RABBIT

- 1 rabbit, jointed (ask your butcher to do this for you)
- 1 tablespoon caraway seeds
- 1 onion, roughly chopped
- 100 ml (3½ fl oz/scant ½ cup) white wine vinegar
- 2 tablespoons plain (all-purpose) flour
- rapeseed oil, for frying
- 100 g (3½ oz) pitted prunes, halved
- 250 ml (8 fl oz/1 cup) beer
- 2 tablespoons soured cream
- salt and white pepper, to taste

First clean the rabbit: soak the pieces in a bowl of warm water with a teaspoon of salt in it for 30 minutes.

Remove the meat from the bowl and pat it dry then massage in the caraway seeds and scatter over the chopped onion. Wrap in a clean tea towel soaked with the vinegar and place it in a baking tray in the fridge to marinate for at least 4 hours (overnight if possible).

When you are ready to start cooking, preheat the oven to 150°C (300°F/gas 2). Unwrap the pieces of meat and dust with the flour. Heat a little rapeseed oil in a frying pan (skillet) over a medium heat and fry the rabbit pieces for a few minutes until browned on all sides.

Transfer the browned rabbit pieces to a lidded casserole dish and add the prunes and beer. Cook in the oven for 1 hour, turning the pieces over from time to time. About 15 minutes before the end of cooking, season with salt and pepper.

Remove the meat from the casserole and leave to stand, covered, for 7–8 minutes. Add the soured cream to the sauce. Portion the rabbit between plates and then pour the casserole sauce over the rabbit to serve.

{Time: 1 hour 30 minutes, plus marinating time}

A breaded escalope (scallop) has been my favourite way to eat meat since I was a child. It appears that I'm not alone in this – it is so popular around the world that it's difficult to pinpoint its exact origins. Some would argue that the discovery of the schnitzel came to Eastern Europe at the exact moment that Józef Radecki, a Czech nobleman and Austrian general, ate one in Milan in the 18th Century and mentioned the recipe in the margin of a military report as a sidenote; others would say that it's origins lie with the Ashkenazi Jews from Germany. **{Serves 5}**

BREADED TURKEY ESCALOPE WITH CUCUMBER AND DILL SALAD

FOR THE CUCUMBER AND DILL SALAD

1 cucumber, peeled
1 medium shallot
1 tablespoon lemon juice
120 ml (4 fl oz/½ cup) soured cream
½ teaspoon caster (superfine) sugar
1 tablespoon freshly chopped dill
salt and white pepper

FOR THE ESCALOPES (SCALLOPS)

2 turkey breasts
1 garlic clove, crushed
2 eggs, beaten
1 tablespoon plain (all-purpose) flour
50 g (1¾ oz/⅓ cup) fine fresh breadcrumbs
2 tablespoons salted butter
salt and white pepper, to taste

First make the salad as it needs some time to 'bite together'. Slice the cucumber and shallot as thinly as you can. Pour the lemon over the sliced cucumber and shallot and season with salt and white pepper. Mix together the soured cream, sugar and dill and add to the cucumber and shallot; toss gently to combine.

Place the turkey breasts in a plastic food bag and bash them with a rolling pin to flatten them and tenderise the meat – you want them to be about 1 cm (½ in) thick.

Mix the salt and pepper into the crushed garlic to make a paste and massage this into the meat. Pour the beaten eggs into a wide, shallow bowl. Mix the flour and the breadcrumbs together and place them on a wide plate. Dip the escalopes in the egg then the breadcrumb-flour mixture.

Melt the butter in a frying pan (skillet) over a medium heat. Once it is sizzling, add the escalopes and fry them for 7–8 minutes on each side, until crisp and golden.

Serve with the cucumber and dill salad on top or on the side, as you prefer.

{Time: 40 minutes}

NOTE: THE AZTEC GUAJALOTE = TURKEY – IS A ABORIGIN NATIVE MEXICAN bird

Liver is incredibly good for you, with practically no fat and plenty of iron, absolutely delicious when prepared well and cheap as chips! What's not to love? *Ćwikła* is the name for beetroot and horseradish paired together. Make the salad first, to give it time to 'bite together'. If you can make the salad the day before, that would be even better! **{Serves 2}**

CHARRED LAMBS' LIVER WITH HORSERADISH-BEETROOT ĆWIKŁA

FOR THE SPICY BEETROOT (BEET) SALAD

¼ teaspoon salt
½ teaspoon caster (superfine) sugar
1 tablespoon red wine vinegar
½ teaspoon cumin seeds, toasted
4 tablespoons horseradish sauce
5 cooked beetroots (beet), peeled and roughly grated

FOR THE CHARRED LAMBS' LIVER

50 g (1¾ oz/3½ tablepsoons) salted butter
1 shallot, finely chopped
200 g (7 oz) lamb's liver, chopped into bite-sized pieces
1 tablespoon balsamic vinegar
salt and white pepper, to taste
ground black pepper

First make the beetroot salad. Stir the sugar and salt into the vinegar until dissolved, then add the cumin seeds (reserving half a teaspoon for the top of the salad) and horseradish sauce. Pour over the cooled, grated beetroot and mix well together. Sprinkle the reserved cumin seeds over the top. Place in the fridge to chill while you prepare the liver.

Melt half the butter in a frying pan (skillet) over a low heat and gently fry the shallot for about 20 minutes – when the edges start becoming crispy, remove the shallot from the pan.

Add a knob of the remaining butter to the pan and fry the liver over a high heat for about 1½ minutes on each side, shaking the pan from time to time while it's cooking.

Add the shallot back to the pan with the liver and fry together for no longer than 30–40 seconds – you want the liver to remain pink in the middle.

Remove the liver and shallot from the pan and allow them to rest for a few moments, covered, while you melt the last of the butter in the pan. Once it's sizzling, add the vinegar, some freshly ground black pepper and simmer so that it reduces slightly.

Pour this sauce over the liver and serve immediately with the salad on the side and perhaps some crusty bread.

{Time: 25 minutes, plus chilling time}

Zrazy is one of those dishes you hear about when Polish people talk of the past. I have always imagined that it was a dish that people used to eat at intellectual dinners while talking about the state of the country, art and poetry.

If you do not have any dried mushrooms, use a cup of good-quality chicken stock instead and fry a few sliced button (white) mushrooms in butter then add them to the casserole with the wine. **{Serves 2}**

BEEF AND GHERKIN OLD COUNTRY ZRAZY

2 x 150 g (5 oz) braising steaks
4 tablespoons Dijon mustard (per steak)
2–3 gherkins, cut into strips the size of a little finger
1 red (bell) pepper, cut into strips the size of a little finger
4–5 dried mushrooms, washed and soaked in hot water overnight (water reserved)
250 ml (8 fl oz/1 cup) red wine
1 slice rye bread (stale is fine)
1 bay leaf
4–5 allspice berries
salt and white pepper, to taste

Place the meat in a plastic food bag or between layers of cling film (plastic wrap) and bash with a rolling pin so that it's very thin and easy to roll.

Smear a good layer of mustard on one side of each steak, then cut each one in half to create four pieces (two *zrazy* for each person).

Place your filling of gherkins and red peppers in the middle of your steaks and fold the beef around it, keeping the roll in place with two or three toothpicks. Place each roll into a flameproof casserole dish and add the rehydrated mushrooms, along with their soaking liquid, red wine, slice of rye bread, bay leaf and the berries. Season well with salt and white pepper.

Place the casserole dish over a medium heat and bring to a simmer, then reduce the heat right down, cover and cook for 2½ hours (if you are short on time you can reduce the cooking time to 2 hours minimum). You'll need to top up the liquid every now and then as it reduces down, using either water or wine.

Serve with mashed potatoes, crusty bread or toasted buckwheat groats.

{Time: 2 hours 30 minutes, plus soaking time}

FISH

"JEDNA Z NAJWAŻNIEJSZYCH CĘCH KUCHNI STĄROPOLSKIEJ BYŁA DUŻA ILOŚĆ I WIELKIE ZRÓŻNICOWANIE DAŃ RYBNYCH. POLSKĄ KUCHNIE CENIONO W EUROPIE WŁASNIE ZA BARDZO ROZWINIĘTĄ SZTUKĘ PRZYRZĄDZANIA POTRAW RYBNYCH."

"One of the most important attributes of old Polish cuisine was the large quantity and variety of its fish dishes. Polish cuisine was valued in Europe precisely because it was so well developed in the art of cooking fish."

{Jaroslaw Dumanowski, Andrzej Pawlas, Jerzy Poznański}

Poland's oldest existing cookbook was written in 1682 by Stanislaw Czerniecki and contains over 100 recipes for fish. In the 17th and 18th Centuries Polish chefs were famous all over Europe for their freshwater fish recipes. To this day, fish is a big part of the Polish diet, prepared and eaten in many different ways – cold, warm, preserved, smoked, jellied, fried, baked and poached. We are not just limited to the fish available in supermarkets – if it's swimming in the sea, lake or river, then we'll eat it. In the summer, this often means simply rolling it in a mixture of flour and breadcrumbs, then frying it in butter to be eaten right there and then, with a *surówka* (slaw) and bread, overlooking the water it inhabited and washing it down with a cold beer.

The Catholic religious calendar, which is an ingrained part of Polish culture and life, whatever our religious beliefs now are, alternates times of fasting with times of feasting. Times of fasting call for fish opposed to meat and this is the main way in which we still fast. In the past the fasting was stricter (almost half the year was spent fasting) and during these times, men would often use the line *'Idę na małą rybkę'*, which translates as 'I'm going out to eat a little fish'. Which has now become a running joke, because the real intention was to wash the fish down with plenty of vodka.

In the colder months, preserved and smoked fish take centre stage. Smoked eel is a personal favourite, though quite rare to come by these days. Carp is always somewhere in the vicinity as I discovered when searching for fresh fish for this book. Our love of carp has been well publicised in the UK, with naughty Poles fishing for this most beloved fish in well-stocked British parks and offering anglers cash for their winning carp (always politely refused in the UK as the carp is always dropped back into the river).

In this chapter, I've tried to demonstrate a variety of fish recipes, inspired by quite distinct regions of Poland as well as including different types of fish. After all, if there is a demand for more freshwater fish then it will be stocked in shops and a great, positive change could come about as a result. (We should never underestimate our power as consumers.) I recommend using a good fishmonger and buying fish that's as local as possible to where you live. There are many rare, exotic treasures to be found, so the most sensible option does not necessarily mean sticking to what you are familiar with. Cooking more unusual varieties means that you are less likely to be eating something that is over-fished; it is also less likely to be farmed in dirty, overcrowded waters.

Sorrel is one of my favourite things to forage for in Poland. It always reminds me of a particular, summer's day a few years ago, when both my grandmas were still alive. For lunch we had decided to make a cold *chłodnik* soup out of foraged sorrel. My mother and I climbed across the wooden planks that separated the tracks next to our house and the field. Once across we walked around, finding the best batches of sorrel. It was a hot, humid day, therefore I felt gleefully lucky when I not only found a brilliant patch of sorrel, but also a little seat right next to it. That is, until I realised I had sat on an ant nest! **{Serves 2}**

BAKED TROUT WITH SORREL SAUCE

2 tablespoons salted butter
100 g (3½ oz) sorrel, washed and finely chopped
100 ml (3½ fl oz/scant ½ cup) fish or vegetable stock
2 small whole trout, cleaned and gutted
1 tablespoon olive oil
1 tablespoon lemon juice
2 tablespoons plain (all-purpose) flour
2 tablespoons crème fraîche
salt and white pepper, to taste

Melt half the butter in a frying pan (skillet) over a low-medium heat and fry the sorrel. When it has wilted, add the stock and cook, covered, for about 20 minutes.

While the sorrel is cooking, preheat the oven to 180°C (350°F/gas 4) and line a baking tray with baking paper (parchment paper).

Place the trout on the prepared baking tray and drizzle with the olive oil. Season well with salt and pepper and then bake in the oven for 20 minutes.

When the sorrel is cooked transfer to a food processor or blender, add the lemon juice and blend to a paste (do the same if using sorrel from a jar).

Melt the remaining butter in a pan over a low-medium heat and add the flour. Stir together and cook for a minute or two to make a roux. Stir in the sorrel mixture and season to taste. Simmer and reduce for roughly 10 minutes, then taste and adjust the seasoning.

Serve the baked trout with this sauce on the side, with a dollop of crème fraîche in the middle.

{Time: 40 minutes}

Mackerel is one of the more sustainable fish on the market, as well as one of the most healthy – as a general rule oily fish tend to have a lot more nutritional value than delicate white fish. However, it does need strong flavours to complement it. I find the flavours of wild cherry – also known as sour cherry – and cinnamon stand up well to the strong tasting mackerel. If you can't get hold of wild cherries, then you can use normal cherries and replace the balsamic vinegar with lemon juice. **{Serves 2}**

BAKED MACKEREL WITH WILD CHERRIES

2 mackerels, cleaned and gutted
rapeseed oil, for drizzling
100 g (3½ oz) wild cherries, pitted (if unavailable use normal cherries and add 2 tablespoons of lemon juice)
¼ teaspoon ground cinnamon
1 tablespoon balsamic vinegar
salt and black pepper, to taste

Preheat the oven to 200°C (400°F/gas 6).

Place the mackerel on a baking tray lined with baking paper (parchment paper), drizzle with rapeseed oil and season well with salt and pepper, massaging it well both inside and outside the fish.

Combine the cherries and ground cinnamon in a bowl, season lightly with salt and pepper and pour over the balsamic vinegar. Stuff the insides of the mackerel with the mixture and use toothpicks to hold the filling inside. Scatter any remaining cherries around the fish.

Bake in the oven for 25 minutes until the top of the mackerel is crisp.

{Time: 45 minutes, plus prepping time}

I always think of halibut as the princess of the fish world, which is why I poach it in Cava. This sauce is a fail-safe; it is ideal for uninspired days as it's very simple and works well with all white fish. If you have white fish in your fridge or freezer and just a few basic ingredients then you can create a winning dish in hardly any time at all. I prefer using delicate white pepper in this recipe, but you may prefer freshly ground black pepper to finish this dish off, or perhaps a bit of both, I leave that choice entirely up to you. **{Serves 2}**

POACHED HALIBUT IN BUTTERY DILL SAUCE

200 ml (7 fl oz/scant 1 cup) Cava or Prosecco
1 bay leaf
1 sprig of rosemary
few celery leaves
few black peppercorns
1 teaspoon lemon zest
2 x 150–180 g (5–6⅓ oz) halibut fillets, about each
2 tablespoons salted butter
handful of finely chopped dill
1 tablespoon lemon juice
salt and white pepper, to taste

Put the Cava in a pan along with the bay leaf, rosemary, celery leaves, peppercorns, lemon zest and a bit of salt and place over a medium-high heat.

Once your poaching liquid is scalding hot (but not boiling), lower in the halibut fillets, reduce the heat and allow to poach over a very low heat for 5–7 minutes. The liquid should nearly cover the fillets.

Meanwhile, make the dill sauce: melt the butter in a pan over a medium heat and add the dill (fresh or frozen works equally well here), lemon juice and season with salt and white pepper.

Remove the halibut fillets from the Cava just as carefully as when you first slid them in and place them in the frying pan with the sauce. Spoon the sauce over the top of the fish and serve with green beans.

{Time: 20 minutes}

The small, ancient town of Toruń, in northern Poland, is famous for its gingerbread. Fittingly, Toruń resembles a gingerbread town, as all of the architecture looks slightly reminiscent of the witch's house in the story of Hansel and Gretel. In this recipe I want to take you on a culinary journey to Toruń, the home of the best gingerbread in Poland. **{Serves 2–3}**

GINGERBREAD SALMON SALAD

- 10 new potatoes, cooked, halved and cooled
- 150 g (5 oz) green beans, cooked
- handful of chopped fresh parsley
- 1 tablespoon plain (all-purpose) flour
- 1 egg, beaten
- 4 tablespoons gingerbread crumbs (see page 252)
- 2 x 200–220 g (7–7½ oz) salmon fillets, cut into 2.5 cm (1 in) cubes
- 1 tablespoon unsalted butter

FOR THE VINAIGRETTE

- 4 tablespoons good-quality olive oil
- 2 tablespoons lemon juice
- 1 teaspoon Sarepska or Dijon mustard
- ½ teaspoon white pepper
- salt, to taste

First make the vinaigrette. Put all the ingredients in a jar with a tight-fitting lid and shake well to combine.

Put the cooled potatoes, green beans and parsley in a serving dish, pour over the vinaigrette and toss to combine.

Tip the flour into a shallow bowl, the beaten egg into another and the gingerbread crumbs into a third. Dip the salmon cubes first in the flour, then the egg and finally the breadcrumbs.

Melt the butter in a frying pan (skillet) over a medium heat and fry the fish for about 8 minutes, turning regularly, until the cubes are crisp and golden on every side.

Serve the gingerbread fish cubes on top of the potato salad.

{Time: 30 minutes}

The prehistoric looking pike is a popular fish in Poland and even more so in neighbouring Lithuania. Pike fillets still have some bones in them and you need to remove these bones with tweezers. If you steam the pike first – it makes the bones stick out just enough to perform this fiddly procedure. In this recipe, as well as in life, the virtue of patience comes in handy. **{Serves 2}**

FRESHWATER PIKE WITH HERBY KASZA

200 g (7 oz) toasted buckwheat groats
2 x 120–140 g (4–5 oz) pike fillets (if unavailable do use gurnard, bluefish or sablefish, but bake for an additional 5-7 minutes)
80 g (3 oz) bacon lardons
1 tablespoon salted butter
handful of fresh parsley, chopped
squeeze of lemon juice
black pepper, to taste

Preheat the oven to 180°C (350°F/gas 4).

Bring a pan of salted water to the boil (twice the volume of the groats) and add the toasted buckwheat groats. Cover, reduce the heat and cook for about 15 minutes. At the same time put the pike fillets in a steaming basket and place on top of the pan of groats; the fish will absorb the flavour of the groats as it steams. Remove the fish after 5 minutes. Then remove any bones from the pike fillets: run your finger over the fish to feel for any bones, then pull them out delicately but firmly with a pair of tweezers.

Meanwhile, fry the lardons in a dry frying pan (skillet) for about 5 minutes, or until they have released some oil. Set aside.

When the *kasza* are cooked, drain them and add them to the lardon pan. Stir the butter and parsley into the hot *kasza* and then transfer to an ovenproof dish. Place the pike on top of the *kasza* and scatter the fried lardons over the top. Season with pepper and bake in the oven for about 15 minutes.

Squeeze the lemon over the top just before serving.

{Time: 45 minutes}

The people of sea-facing Pomerania are by their very nature experts in the art of preparing sea fish. Their land is sandy and infertile, yet the cold Baltic more than compensates for the earth's lack, acting as a sea garden which provides many delicious foodstuffs. Flounder is a flaky, flat fish that lives at the bottom of the sea and its flavour is not too dissimilar from shellfish. It goes sublimely well with the strong flavours of tangy apple and earthy almonds. **{Serves 2}**

FLOUNDER BAKED WITH APPLES AND ALMONDS POMERANIAN STYLE

2 tablespoons salted butter, softened
1 large flounder or 2 small ones, cleaned and gutted (if unavailable you can use turbot or fluke)
1 apple, peeled, cored and chopped
2 tablespoons flaked (slivered) almonds
½ lemon, quartered into 4
salt and black pepper, to taste

Preheat the oven to 150°C (300°F/gas 2).

Rub the butter all over the flounder and place it on a large baking tray lined with baking paper (parchment paper). Scatter the apple pieces around the fish and bake in the oven for 15 minutes.

Sprinkle the flaked almonds over the fish and season well with salt and pepper. Return to the oven for a further 10 minutes.

Serve with lemon wedges.

{Time: 30 minutes}

Sprats are delicious battered and deep-fried (what isn't?). They are a bigger, meatier form of whitebait but I recommend cutting their heads off. This dish is simple yet evocative and it makes you feel as though you are not too far away from a warm beach. **{Serves 4}**

BEER-BATTERED CRISPY SPRATS WITH PAPRIKA MAYONNAISE

100 g (3½ oz/generous ¾ cup) plain (all-purpose) flour
1 teaspoon garlic salt
50–75 ml (2–3 fl oz/scant ¼–⅓ cup) beer
400 g (14 oz) sprats, heads removed (if unavailable do use fresh anchovies or baby sardines)
200 ml (7 fl oz/scant 1 cup) rapeseed oil
½ teaspoon sweet paprika
salt and white pepper, to taste
3 tablespoons mayonnaise
lemon wedges, to serve

First make the batter. Mix half the flour, the garlic salt and some white pepper in a bowl. Start whisking in the beer until you reach the consistency of a very thick, gloopy milkshake.

Place the remaining flour in a shallow bowl and dust the sprats with it. Meanwhile, pour the oil into a heavy-based deep pan and place over a medium-high heat – you should have about 2.5 cm (1 in) of oil in the pan.

Dip the flour-dusted sprats in the batter and then fry them in the hot oil, in batches. Make sure the oil is hot enough – a drop of batter should sizzle and turn golden as soon as it hits the oil. Gently lower the sprats in by their tails, making sure you don't splash yourself. Fry for a couple of minutes, until the sprats are crisp and golden.

Whisk the paprika into the mayonnaise. Drain the sprats on kitchen paper and season with salt. Serve with lemon wedges to squeeze over and the paprika-mayonnaise to dip into.

{Time: 25 minutes}

I was never a huge fan of Poland's favourite fish, the carp, until I met Pan Waldek. Pan Waldek lives on a magical farm next to his two fishing ponds, with his wife, son and cow. We asked him to try and catch us a pike, but the pike wouldn't bite. The carp did luckily, so we drove to the next village to pick it up from him. Upon arrival we were sat down in the shade and given carp *rosół* prepared by Waldek's wife, followed by his own fried carp. On the side we ate juicy tomatoes and crunchy cucumbers from their garden. Pan Waldek is a great believer in organic farming. He said that his carp were especially good because the ponds were so clean that they didn't even have mosquitoes in them. Pan Waldek's other secret was to marinate the carp for at least an hour in a blend of oregano and salt, with a few bay leaves.

If you would like to try carp, make sure you get it from a good, clean source. Ask your fishmonger to fillet it in two. You can also substitute carp for another fish – a fresh trout, for example, or simply ask your fishmonger what other local fish they would recommend on that particular day. **{Serves 4}**

PAN WALDEK'S OREGANO-FRIED CARP

1 carp fillet (half a carp), about 500 g (1 lb 2 oz) each
2 tablespoons dried oregano
5–6 bay leaves
100 g (3½ oz/generous ¾ cup) plain (all-purpose) flour
100 g (3½ oz/¾ cup) dried breadcrumbs
rapeseed oil, for frying
salt and white pepper

Massage the fish with a mixture of oregano and salt and pepper. Place the bay leaves at the bottom of a dish and place the fish on top. Leave this to marinate in the fridge for 1–2 hours.

Mix together the flour and breadcrumbs and pour onto a shallow plate or bowl. Place the carp fillets on the plate, turning them over and making sure that they're completely covered in breadcrumbs.

Shallow-fry the rapeseed oil in a frying pan over a high heat. Once the oil is hot (a few breadcrumbs should sizzle as soon as they hit the oil), add the carp and fry until golden brown and crunchy, about 3–4 minutes each side.

Serve immediately with bread or fries and plenty of slaws or *surówka* (see pages 139).

{Time: 20 minutes, plus marinating time}

VEGETABLES, BEANS AND KASZA

"…Row on row
Of fruit trees give their shade to beds below
cabbage sits and bows her scrawny pate
Musing upon her vegetable fate;
The slender bean entwines the carrot's tresses
And with a thousand eyes his love expresses;
Here hangs the golden tassel of the maize,
And there a bellied watermelon strays,
That rolling from his stem far off is found,
A stranger on the crimson beetroot's ground."

{Adam Mickiewicz, Pan Tadeusz}

Polish cuisine is rarely thought of as being rich in healthy vegetables, yet in reality there are many vegetable dishes and vegetarian options. One word for vegetables is *włoszczyzna*, which comes from the word *Włochy* – the Polish word for Italy. This is thanks to the famous Italian Queen Bona Sforza who brought many vegetables to Poland during her reign.

Generally, when people think of Poland potatoes spring to mind, and I must confess we do love the common spud! When I was little I'd put them in the bottom of a fire pit. Once the sun had gone down and the fire had burned out, the spud was retrieved from the bottom of the pit – coal black and cooked through. You'd open up this black charcoal ball to reveal the fluffy white flesh that tasted of the earth and the fire, all it needed was some butter and salt. To get the full wonder of this, the simplest of dishes; the potato had to be organic, and not too old.

However, it is not the potato, but *kasza* (pronounced 'kasha') that is the original food of our Slavic ancestors. *Kasza* is the word we use for many different grains, each one with its own flavour, nutrients and uses. *Kasza* has been cultivated in Central Eastern Europe since the first Slavic settlers came and farmed the land, around the beginning of the first millennium. During those pagan times, it was given as a gift to the gods, along with honey and cheese, to ensure a healthy, successful life of a newborn child. The traditional way of cooking *kasza* is boiling it in water for about 20 minutes, like rice, but then wrapping the pan up in newspaper, tying a towel round it and sticking the whole package under a duvet, for another hour, in order to steam. One of my clearest childhood memories is my grandma Ziuta wrapping the *kasza* up like a baby in a towel and a blanket, then putting it in her bed for the best part of an hour, in what seemed to be a ritualistic rite. (You can also just leave it covered to carry on steaming for half an hour. However, this loving method does produce the best tasting buckwheat groats.)

Kaszas, like beans, are dried and are available year round, whereas vegetable dishes are usually seasonal, meaning we eat different vegetables at different times of the year. The firm favourite *kasza* in Poland has to be the dark brown, toasted buckwheat groats, *kasza gryczana*. Although it was considered peasant food for a very long time, the Transylvanian King Batory, through sheer love of this *kasza*, elevated it from the peasants' table to the King's table. The popular Polish-Hungarian Queen Jadwiga favoured *kasza krakowska*, which she apparently ate sweetened with raisins. Even though Queen Jadwiga generously gave up all her jewels to expand the national university, it was rumoured that she kept her precious dried fruits and exotic spices under lock and key in a chest reserved for treasure – that's my kind of Queen!

Even though the concept of vegetarianism is a relatively new idea to this part of the world, I find that many of these dishes can be prepared without meat. When there is meat in a vegetable dish you can leave it out or make simple substitutions to ensure the dish is entirely vegetarian-friendly.

My perpetually young-at-heart great auntie Krysia was my grandma Halinka's younger sister, who lived in Olsztyn, not too far from the magical, meandering lake district called Mazury. She's been making this potato pie for years, therefore the quantities and instructions she gave to me were 'lots of marjoram, lots, lots' and 'a good amount of bacon, but not too much'. Here, I give you my interpretation of this delicious, family recipe. **{Serves 8}**

MELT-IN-YOUR-MOUTH MAZURIAN POTATO MARJORAM PIE

- 1.5 kg (3 lb 5 oz) floury (mealy) potatoes, such as Maris Piper or King Edward (Yukon Gold)
- 150 g (5 oz) bacon lardons or finely chopped bacon
- 2 tablespoons rapeseed oil
- 2 onions, very finely chopped
- 2 garlic cloves, crushed
- 2 eggs, separated
- 1 tablespoon plain (all-purpose) flour
- 3 tablespoons double (heavy) cream
- 1 tablespoon dried marjoram
- salt and white and black pepper, to taste

NOTE: LATE 14c. SPANISH INVATION TO THE AMERICAS STARTED, GOLD, SILVER, METHALS " POURING TO ALL EUROPE. AS WELL, NOT KNOWN TO THEM, ALL KINDS OF VEGETABLES AND FRUITS, SPANIARDS AND POTATOS CAME 1ST. TO IRELAND, THEN, TO ALL OVER THE WORLD, AND BACK TO NORTH AMERICA WITH THE IRIS IMMIGRANTS. THEREFORE THEIR FOREIGN NAMES. AS M. P. K.E, ETC.

Preheat the oven to 180°C (350°F/gas 4) and liberally grease an 900 g (2 lb) loaf tin.

Grate the potatoes as finely as you can. If the potatoes are watery, then you will need to squeeze out some of the excess water. Place the grated potato in a large bowl.

Fry the lardons or bacon bits in a frying pan over a medium heat until they release their fat and turn crispy then set aside on a plate. Add the oil to the frying pan over a medium heat and fry the onions for about 5 minutes, until softened. Add the garlic and continue to fry for 2–3 minutes. Allow both to cool for 5–10 minutes before adding to the grated potato.

Beat the egg whites until soft and fluffy and then add the egg yolks and beat together until combined. Stir the eggs into the grated potato mixture, then add the flour and cream.

Add the marjoram and season the mixture with a large pinch of salt and both the peppers (be liberal). As the bacon is salty you need only add 2 pinches of salt, however, if you were to make a vegetarian version and substitute the bacon for mushrooms, then you may want to add a little more.

Tip the mixture into your prepared dish, the depth of the *babka* needs to be at least 8 cm (3 in) and bake in the oven for 50 minutes–1 hour, it is ready when the top is golden and crisp on the top.

{Time: 1 hour 25 minutes}

Beetroot could well be Eastern Europe's favourite vegetable – we eat a lot of it, especially during the winter. This dish originated in the Jewish communities of Eastern Europe using our favourite vegetable in a rather charming way, its deep flavour is complemented by the creamy garlicky bread sauce. You can use slightly stale, dry bread for this sauce. **{Serves 4}**

ROAST BEETROOT SLICES WITH WHITE BREAD SAUCE

500 g (1 lb 2 oz) beetroot (beet), scrubbed
75–100 ml (2½–3½ fl oz/ scant ½ cup) olive oil, plus extra for drizzling
1 tablespoon dried thyme
juice of 1 lemon
4 slices white bread, crusts removed
2 garlic cloves, chopped
½ teaspoon garlic granules
salt and white pepper, to taste

Preheat the oven to 180°C (350°F/gas 4).

Place the beetroot in a roasting tin, drizzle with olive oil and sprinkle over some salt and the thyme. Roast in the oven for 45 minutes, or until tender.

Meanwhile, mix together the olive oil and lemon juice in a shallow bowl and soak the bread slices in it for 30–40 minutes.

When the beetroot is cooked through allow to cool slightly before peeling off the skin and cutting into slices. Arrange over a serving plate (a fan shape looks nice).

When the bread has finished soaking, place the bread, olive oil and lemon juice in a food processor or blender, along with the garlic cloves, garlic granules and some seasoning. Whizz until you have a smooth sauce.

Serve the sauce alongside the roasted beetroot, as it functions as a dipping sauce.

{Time: 1 hour}

My mother is the true hero of this book, as many of the dishes I have shared with you are ones that she has passed on to me (and indeed her mother passed down to her).

This creamy side dish is all about the taste of the carrots, so you need to use the best quality carrots you can find – the young, thin ones with the green tops have the most flavour. **{Serves 4}**

MAMA'S PEAS AND CARROT CUBES

300–350 g (10 oz) carrots, peeled and cut into dice
150 g (5 oz) peas, defrosted if frozen
25 g (1 oz/2 tablespoons) salted butter
1 tablespoon plain (all-purpose) flour
50 ml (2 fl oz/scant ¼ cup) milk
salt and white pepper, to taste

Put the diced carrots in a pan and pour over just enough boiling water to cover by about 1 cm (½ in). Place over a medium heat and cook until almost soft. Add the peas and simmer together for about 5 minutes.

Meanwhile, melt the butter in a pan over a medium heat. Add the flour and cook, stirring, for a couple of minutes. Gradually add the milk, stirring all the time to make a thick, smooth sauce.

Add this *zasmażka* sauce to the pan of vegetables. Stir it in thoroughly, season to taste and allow it to heat through and thicken for about 2 minutes before serving.

{Time: 25 minutes}

Many old Romany gypsy communities travelled through these lands over the ages, some settling along their way. As a child, I was attracted to their way of life: their primal connection to the earth, sitting around a fire every night, their nomadic existence, the cosy caravans full of trinkets and, of course, the clothes. This particular sweet-and-ever-so-slightly-spicy sauce is known as a gypsy-style sauce throughout Poland. **{Serves 2 as a main course}**

GYPSY-STYLE MIXED GREENS

FOR THE GREENS

150 g (5 oz) green beans
150 g (5 oz) tenderstem broccoli
2 courgettes (zucchini), cut into strips

FOR THE SAUCE

1 onion, chopped
1 red (bell) pepper, roughly chopped
2 garlic cloves
4–5 large fresh tomatoes, chopped
olive oil, for drizzling
1 teaspoon sweet paprika
½ teaspoon chilli powder
1 teaspoon dried marjoram
1 teaspoon Dijon mustard
1 teaspoon honey
25 g (1 oz/2 tablespoons) unsalted butter
50 g (1¾ oz) mushrooms, very finely chopped
salt and black pepper, to taste
shaved Pecorino or Parmesan, to serve

First prepare the sauce. Preheat the oven to 200°C (400°F/gas 6).

Put the onion, pepper, garlic and tomatoes into a roasting tin, drizzle with olive oil and sprinkle over the paprika, chilli powder, marjoram and some salt and pepper. Roast for about 30 minutes, until ever so slightly charred.

Make sure all the green are cut into uniform lengths (about the length of a green bean) and steam gently for 10 minutes while you finish preparing the sauce.

Tip all the roasted vegetables into a food processor and pulse briefly before adding the mustard and honey. Pulse again to combine (you are looking for a chunky texture). Taste and adjust the seasoning and then transfer to a pan.

Melt the butter in a frying pan (skillet) over a medium heat and fry the mushrooms until golden brown. Add to the sauce and simmer gently for a couple of minutes until heated through.

Serve the steamed greens with the sauce over the top and a few shavings of Pecorino.

{Time: 45 minutes}

Beans are the kind of wholesome fare that are good for the soul and the digestive system. *Fasolka po bretońsku*, as these beans are called in Polish – are earthy and full of flavour, delicious eaten with fresh, crusty bread and nothing else. *Fasola jaś* – the type of large, white beans we traditionally use for this recipe – are difficult to come by in many countries, but butter beans are similar and work very well indeed. If you have time, use dried beans and soak them in cold water overnight; otherwise if you want to prepare a quick supper, the ones out of a can work just fine. **{Serves 2}**

EVERY bean VARIETY COMES FROM MEXICO AND SOUTH AMÉRICA

BUTTER BEANS IN A MARJORAM AND TOMATO BROTH

If you are using soaked dried beans, drain and rinse them and then cook them in a large pan of boiling, salted water for about 35 minutes, or until soft (but not falling apart).

Meanwhile, heat the oil in a large pan over a medium heat and fry the onion and bacon for about 5 minutes, stirring occasionally, until the onion is softened. Stir in the marjoram and paprika and cook for a further minute or two.

Once they're glossy, add the chopped tomatoes and the now cooked and drained butter beans (or canned beans). Allow to simmer for 20 minutes, stirring occasionally, before serving with some crusty bread.

{Time: 1 hour if using dried beans, 25 minutes if canned}

- 400 g (14 oz/2¼ cups) dried butter (lima) beans, soaked overnight (or 2 x 400 g/14 oz cans, rinsed and drained)
- 2 tablespoons rapeseed oil
- 1 onion, roughly chopped
- 6 rashers (slices) streaky (lean) bacon, chopped
- 1 tablespoon dried marjoram
- 1 teaspoon paprika
- 1 x 100 g (14 oz) can chopped tomatoes
- salt and white and black pepper, to taste

{Herby Chanterelles with *Kasza* Cubes and Lovage for your Sweetheart}

Mushroom picking is a favourite Polish pastime – we have 31 varieties of edible fungi growing wild. They are sold all over the country in autumn, their weathered pickers sitting with their findings in wooden crates at the local markets. This recipe requires untoasted buckwheat groats, which are readily available in supermarkets, usually in the wholefoods section. Lovage, on the other hand, has fallen out of favour in the West, and is not so easy to get hold of. Polish old wives claim you should add lovage or *lubczyk* to the meals cooked for your sweetheart so that they stay in love with you. If you can not get hold of any do use dried thyme instead. **{Serves 4}**

HERBY CHANTERELLES WITH KASZA CUBES AND LOVAGE FOR YOUR SWEETHEART {see page 133}

FOR THE CRISPY KASZA CUBES:

250 g (9 oz) untoasted buckwheat
rapeseed oil, for frying
sea salt

FOR THE HERBY CHANTERELLES:

300 g (10½ oz) wild mushrooms (chanterelles are perfect)
2 tablespoons olive oil
1 garlic clove, chopped
½ teaspoon dried lovage (or dried thyme)
½ teaspoon dried marjoram
250 ml (8 fl oz/1 cup) white wine
250 ml (8 fl oz/1 cup) single (light) cream
handful of picked herbs, to garnish such as thyme, lovage, parsley or lemon balm
salt and black pepper, to taste

First prepare the *kasza*. Pour boiling water over the buckwheat – twice the volume of water to buckwheat. Cook until all the water is absorbed and the *kasza* is soft, which takes about 20 minutes, then allow to steam for a further 10 minutes. Spread the hot *kasza* out on a baking tray moistened with very cold water and pat it down to form an even layer. Leave it in a cool place overnight.

The next day, chop the mushrooms evenly so they are the same size (especially if you are using mixed varieties). Heat the olive oil in a large pan and fry the mushrooms over a medium heat for about 7 minutes, or until browned all over.

Add the garlic, lovage and marjoram and fry, stirring continuously, for a couple of minutes, then stir in the wine and simmer over a low heat for 5 minutes.

Meanwhile, cut the *kasza* into 3 cm (1¼ in) squares. Pour about 1–2 cm (½–1 in) rapeseed oil into a large frying pan (skillet) and place over a medium heat (you need enough oil to create an uninterrupted layer of oil in the pan). When the oil is sizzling hot fry the *kasza* cubes for about 4 minutes on each side until browned. Season with sea salt near the end of the frying time and then drain on kitchen paper.

Add the cream to the mushrooms and stir until heated through. Season to taste and pour over the crispy *kasza* cubes. Scatter with fresh herbs before serving.

{Time: 45 minutes, plus overnight cooling time}

Millet groats, or *kasza jaglana* are an ancient *kasza* that are incredibly nutritious. Traditionally, it's eaten either for breakfast, as a soup similar to *kasza manna*, or used as a side to a meaty sauce, rather like *kasza gryczana* (buckwheat groats). I've re-worked the *kasza* in this recipe into 'falafel'-style veggie balls that make a welcome addition to any fresh salad; I've added lemon balm into this recipe, which is a citrusy, fresh-tasting herb that's sold all around in Poland. It's worth growing the herb yourself, but if you can not get hold of it, feel free to replace it with basil or coriander (cilantro). If you are short on time you can replace the dried chickpeas with canned. **{Serves 4}**

MILLET GROATS FALAFELS WITH A ZINGY GHERKIN, TOMATO AND LEMON BALM SALAD

First make the falafels. If you are using soaked dried chickpeas, drain and rinse them and then cook them in a large pan of boiling, salted water for about 45 minutes, or until soft.

Meanwhile, heat 1 tablespoon of the rapeseed oil in a pan and fry the onion and carrot over a medium heat until softened. Add the millet groats and stir into the carrot and onion until thoroughly combined. Add enough boiling water to cover by about 1 cm (½ in). Cover with a lid and cook over a low heat for about 30 minutes.

For the salad, combine the tomatoes and gherkins (which should be uniform in size) in a bowl and add the chives and lemon balm. Pour the lemon juice and olive oil over the top, season to taste and chill in the fridge for at least 30 minutes.

Continue preparing the falafels. Tip the cooked and drained chickpeas (or canned chickpeas) into a food processor or blender and blitz to a paste. You might need to add a little olive oil or lemon juice if this mixture is very stiff. Transfer to a bowl and combine with the cooked millet groats. Add the paprika to the bowl, then allow the mixture to cool before adding the egg. Mix all the ingredients thoroughly with your hands and then roll into small walnut-size balls.

Tip the breadcrumbs onto a large plate and then roll each falafel in the breadcrumbs. Heat the remaining rapeseed oil in a frying pan (skillet) over a medium heat. Fry the balls in batches, until lightly browned on each side. Transfer to an ovenproof dish.

Preheat the grill (broiler) to high. Scatter the grated goat's cheese over the top of the balls and grill (broil) for 2 minutes, or until the cheese melts. Serve on top of the zingy salad.

{Time: 1 hour 45 minutes, if using dried chickpeas or 1 hour if using canned chickpeas}

FOR THE 'FALAFELS'

100 g (3½ oz/½ cup) dried chickpeas, soaked overnight (or ½ x 400 g/14 oz can, rinsed and drained)
4 tablespoons rapeseed oil
1 small onion, finely chopped
1 carrot, finely grated
100 g (3½ oz) millet groats, rinsed and drained
½ teaspoon paprika
1 egg
50 g (1¾ oz/⅓ cup) dried breadcrumbs
50–75 g (1¾–2¾ oz/scant ½–⅔ cup) hard goat's cheese, grated

FOR THE SALAD

4 tomatoes, chopped
4 gherkins, chopped
handful of chives, chopped
handful of fresh lemon balm, roughly chopped
3 tablespoons lemon juice
2 tablespoons olive oil
salt and white pepper, to taste

As spring progresses and the earth blooms, fresher tastes start coming into play in Polish cooking. Side dishes begin to require young vegetables – this is especially true of the cabbage, which has a completely different flavour later on in the year. Young cabbage has a sweet taste that can be replicated through the use of another sweet cabbage such as the oblong Napa cabbage at other times of the year. **{Serves 6}**

YOUNG SPRING CABBAGE WITH DILL AND BACON

- 4 tablespoons rapeseed oil
- 200 g (7 oz) streaky (lean) bacon, cut into fine strips
- 2 large onions, finely chopped
- 2 leafy young cabbages or Napa cabbages, shredded
- 2 tablespoons water
- juice of 1 lemon
- 2 bunches of dill, finely chopped
- 3–4 tablespoons tomato purée (paste)
- 1 teaspoon caster (superfine) sugar
- salt and white pepper, to taste

Heat the oil in a large frying pan (skillet) and fry the bacon strips over a medium heat until crispy. Add the onions and continue to fry for a further 4–5 minutes.

Add the shredded cabbage and water and stir together. Season and cover with a lid, reduce the heat to low and cook for 10 minutes.

Stir in the lemon juice, three-quarters of the chopped dill, tomato purée and the sugar. Continue to fry, stirring every couple of minutes, for a further 10 minutes with the lid removed. Try a bit and season again to taste.

Just before serving add the reserved dill. This dish works well as an accompaniment to chicken, or can be eaten on its own with crusty bread.

{Time: 30 minutes}

TWO CLASSIC CRUNCHY SURÓWKA SLAWS FOR FISH

The word *surówka* indicates that the vegetables must be raw (pickled vegetables are also acceptable). The other vital quality of a Polish slaw is that it should 'bite together', in other words, it shouldn't be eaten straight away. Unlike a leafy salad, which goes limp after a couple of hours, a slaw tends to taste better over time. A *surówka* can be different combinations of grated or sliced vegetables and sauces, each Polish household has its own favourites: these are mine.

My father swears by sauerkraut 'juice' (the brine) as a hangover cure and perhaps there's something in it because sauerkraut – or *kapusta kiszona* in Polish – is one of our country's healthiest foods, full of vitamin C and probiotics. **{Serves 4}**

SAUERKRAUT SLAW

2 tablespoon white wine vinegar
½ teaspoon sugar
3 tablespoons olive oil
300 g (10½ oz) sauerkraut (see page 251), drained
2 carrots, grated
1 small onion, very finely chopped
white pepper, to taste

Mix the vinegar and sugar together until the sugar dissolves, then add the oil and some white pepper.

Combine the sauerkraut, carrots and onion together in a bowl and then pour the dressing over the top. Taste and add more pepper if desired, then place in the fridge for at least 30 minutes before serving.

{Time: 10 minutes, plus marinating time}

There are no hard and fast rules as to what kind of fish these slaws should be eaten with, yet I personally think the leek slaw is better suited to white or fried fish. The leeks have a strong flavour, which is tempered by the mayonnaise and yoghurt, whereas the apple brings sweetness to the slaw – it's a winning combination. **{Serves 4}**

LEEK SLAW

2 tablespoons mayonnaise
2 tablespoons Greek yoghurt
2 leeks, finely chopped
1 apple, grated
salt and white pepper, to taste

Combine the mayonnaise and yoghurt together in a bowl and season with salt and white pepper.

Add the chopped leeks and grated apple and mix thoroughly. Chill in the fridge for at least 30 minutes before serving.

{Time: 10 minutes, plus marinating time}

This dish is full of iron, vitamins and protein and is so delicious that you can easily eat a whole plateful. The secret is the garlic and the creamy *zasmażka* (roux). **{Serves 2}**

CREAMY SPINACH PURÉE WITH FRIED EGG

250 g (9 oz) spinach, washed
25 g (1 oz/2 tablespoons) unsalted butter
1 tablespoon plain (all-purpose) flour
2 generous splashes of milk
1 garlic clove, crushed
salt, to taste
1 egg (per person)

Bring a large pan of salted water to a boil and then blanch the spinach for 2 minutes. Drain thoroughly, pressing down on the spinach with the back of a spoon to remove as much water as possible (reserving leftover water for sauce). Chop the spinach to a rough paste.

Melt most of the butter (reserve a little for frying the eggs) in a pan over a medium heat. Add the flour and cook, stirring, for a couple of minutes. Gradually add the milk, stirring all the time to make a thick, smooth paste. Add any juices from the blended spinach to the pan, in order to dilute it and make the sauce less gloopy, then remove from the heat.

Mash the crushed garlic with a little bit of salt (this is a special mixture that's used for many dishes in Poland). Add to the chopped spinach and then tip the spinach mixture into the pan and place over a very low heat. Cook, stirring all the time, for 5 minutes.

Melt the remaining butter in a separate frying pan (skillet) and fry the eggs over a very low heat, covered. The idea is to gently cook the whites while keeping the yolks runny. Season with a little salt and serve the eggs on top of the spinach.

{Time: 20 minutes}

You know those side dishes that you can't leave alone? This is one of them: a sweet-yet-savoury, creamy beetroot purée, which is an ideal side dish to all roast meats. Beetroot is good for the liver, the heart and even thought to prevent the development of certain cancers. The magic is in its dramatic, blood-red colour which stains everything it comes into contact with.

{Serves 4 as a side dish}

BEETROOT PUREE

- 8–10 beetroot (beets), cooked and peeled
- 25 g (1 oz/2 tablespoons) unsalted butter
- 1 tablespoon plain (all-purpose) flour
- 100 ml (3½ fl oz/scant ½ cup) milk
- 1 tablespoon caster (superfine) sugar
- salt, to taste

Finely grate the beetroot so that they turn to mush.

Melt the butter in a pan over a medium heat. Add the flour and cook, stirring, for a couple of minutes. Gradually add the milk, stirring all the time to make a thick, smooth sauce.

Add the grated beetroot and sugar to the pan and stir until well combined and hot. Season to taste with salt and serve.

{Time: 25 minutes}

In Poland, we see the cauliflower as a versatile vegetable that we eat as a side dish, a warm *zakąska* or a creamy soup. This famous dish is simply cauliflower covered in a crispy, golden breadcrumb sauce. I find that the Brussels sprouts are a welcome addition to this dish, as their bitterness offsets the sweetness of the cauliflower. **{Serves 4}**

WARSAW-STYLE CAULIFLOWER WITH BRUSSELS SPROUTS

- 1 small cauliflower, broken up into florets
- 200 g (7 oz) Brussels sprouts, halved lengthways
- 100 g (3½ oz/7 tablespoons) salted butter
- 75 g (2½ oz/1⅓ cups) fresh breadcrumbs

Bring a large pan of lightly salted water to a boil and cook the cauliflower and Brussels sprouts for about 20 minutes, or until tender but still with some bite. (You can also steam the vegetables for the same amount of time.)

Meanwhile, melt the butter in a frying pan (skillet) and fry the breadcrumbs over a low-medium heat until golden. Make sure you don't burn them – if they start turning brown rather than golden then they have gone too far.

Drain the vegetables, tip into a serving bowl and pour over the fried breadcrumbs.

{Time: 20 minutes}

Magda and I met as children in the seaside resort of Jarosławiec. We hit it off immediately, as did our parents, and according to the holiday snaps we spent the remainder of our time in Jarosławiec together. Now in our mid-thirties we still go on little holidays together whenever we get the chance and spend a lot of that time talking about food. Magda is the queen of vegetables, this is her salad, made from young beetroot leaves with the addition of some toasted pumpkin seeds – one of my all-time favourite salad toppings. **{Serves 4}**

MAGDALENA'S BOTWINKA SALAD OF YOUNG BEETROOT LEAVES

8 small new potatoes
25 g (1 oz/2 tablespoons) unsalted butter
large handful of chopped dill
200 g (7 oz) young beetroot (beet) leaves
2 tomatoes, chopped
4 slices of Parma ham (prosciutto)
handful of pumpkin seeds, toasted

FOR THE VINAIGRETTE:
4 tablespoons extra-virgin olive oil
2 tablespoons truffle-infused balsamic vinegar
salt and black pepper, to taste

Cook the new potatoes in boiling, salted water until tender, then drain and combine with the butter and chopped dill.

Meanwhile combine the vinaigrette ingredients in a lidded jam jar and shake well to mix it all together.

Place the young beetroot leaves and chopped tomatoes on a large serving plate and pour over the vinaigrette. Arrange the buttery dill potatoes over the top, followed by the Parma ham. Finish by scattering the toasted pumpkin seeds whimsically over the top.

{Time: 30 minutes}

When they are young, broad beans can just be cooked as they are in boiling, salted water until soft, then served with a knob of butter melting over the top. Later in the summer, when they are older, you just need to slip off their slightly tougher outer skins before eating. This simple sage butter turns them into something quite special. Eat them as a substantial snack or as a light meal with some crusty bread or as a main meal with pork chops. **{Serves 4 as a side}**

BROAD BEANS WITH SAGE BUTTER

Cook the beans in a large pan of boiling, salted water until they are firm but not too soft – and definitely not mushy. This should take about 10–20 minutes (depending on the age of the broad beans) but do check after 15 minutes by tasting a bean.

While they are cooking, melt the butter in a frying pan (skillet) and fry the sage leaves over a medium heat until crispy – this should take about 10 minutes, turning them halfway through cooking.

Once the broad beans are cooked, transfer them to serving dish and pour the sage butter over the top. Season with salt before serving.

{Time: 30 minutes}

400 g (14 oz) broad (fava) beans
50 g (1¾ oz/3½ tablespoons) salted butter
16 fresh sage leaves
salt, to taste

DUMPLINGS

A dozen years ago, at a sit-down wedding event the conversation turned to food. (What else are you going to talk about with a group of strangers on your table?) When a girl scoffed 'isn't Polish food just dumplings?' at some remark I'd made about my Polish culinary preferences. It was in that moment that I became filled with a determination to do something to remedy this common misconception about my homeland's food. I didn't know how I was going to tackle the problem, yet the seed was sown. Although, it's entirely understandable that people don't know much about the rather niche subject of Polish food I wanted to add my offering to the world on the various wonders of Polish cooking.

Although dumplings may not be the most important food to us Poles, we do love them dearly. *Pierogi* are the most universally recognisable of our Polish dumplings yet there are many, many more varieties. Some we use as a carbohydrate base for a main meal, others are a meal in themselves; some are eaten with soups, while others can be eaten as a dessert; some are sweet, while others savoury. There are dumplings that are unique to certain regions, and some that are called by the same name yet eaten differently from area to area. A good example of this is the potato *pyzy*, which in my region, Mazowsze, are usually eaten as UFO-shaped balls with a dent in the middle – this is how my grandma Ziuta used to make them and she was a Mazovian through and through. My grandma Halinka on the other hand, reminisced about stuffed *pyzy* that she used to eat in Lithuania (which I have recreated in this chapter with lamb). *Pierogi* have even more varieties, in the mountains they are stuffed

AFTER THE 15th CENTURY INVATION TO THE NEW WORLD, BY COLON, SPANIARDS AND OTHER EUROPEANS, THE BOUNTY OF NEW FOOD POTATOS, VEGETABLES, FRUITS, GOLD, SILVER, NATURAL INDUSTRIAL PRODUCE LIKE THE CAUCHO (RUBBER) CAME OUT, TO THE WHOLE WORLD. SO IN MORE WAYS THAN ONE, THE ABORIGEN NATIVE PEOPLES OF THE CONTINENT, THE GREAT AGROCULTURIST, MADE YOU ALL WITH THEIR WORK, HEALTHY AND WEALTHY, AND THAT IS NOT NEW FRUITS, VEGETABLES STILL ARE COMING OUT. ALL,

WHAT IS YOUR CONTRIBUTION, IN THAT REGARD, TO THE WORLD.

with buckwheat groats and *bryndza* (a salty, creamy sheep's milk cheese similar to feta), while in other regions it's spiced with meat or sauerkraut and wild mushrooms as a vegetarian option. Come the summer, however, you'll find most parts of the country enjoying both bilberry and strawberry *pierogi*.

Making dumplings is not a precise science – there are many variables such as the size of the eggs, the type of flour, the way you knead, whether or not you leave the dough to rest or not. Although, I give you the precise measurements, I ask you to listen to your inner voice – the inner old Polish housewife – that will tell you to add more water when the dough feels too dry, to cover your hands with flour when the dough is too sticky, to be patient and knead it for a while when it seems like the dough has gone awry, or simply to cover it with a damp cloth and have a rest when you think it's ready.

There are also many different types of *pierogi* dough, not to mention different ways of preparing the same dough. But when it comes to classic *pierogi* dough one method is not necessarily better than another. Adding eggs to the mixture is the way most Polish people would make *pierogi* nowadays, yet this was not the original method. Old-style Polish dough used to be made from flour and butter – no eggs – but due to the Italian influence on our cuisine over hundreds of years, eggs replaced butter as the binding agent. I use both in the recipes in this chapter, but if you run out of eggs, then you can experiment with adding more butter. All in all, I find dumplings to be quite forgiving and even if the result isn't perfect they will still leave you feeling very satisfied that you made them yourself.

MAKING DUMPLINGS

Dumplings are incredibly simple to make and very much part of our Polish heritage, all you need is a little confidence in the art of folding and preparing the dough, to make these little wonders. Once mastered, dumplings can be made in minimal time and truly are little flavour bombs that you can fill with whatever mixture your heart desires!

PIEROGI METHOD 1

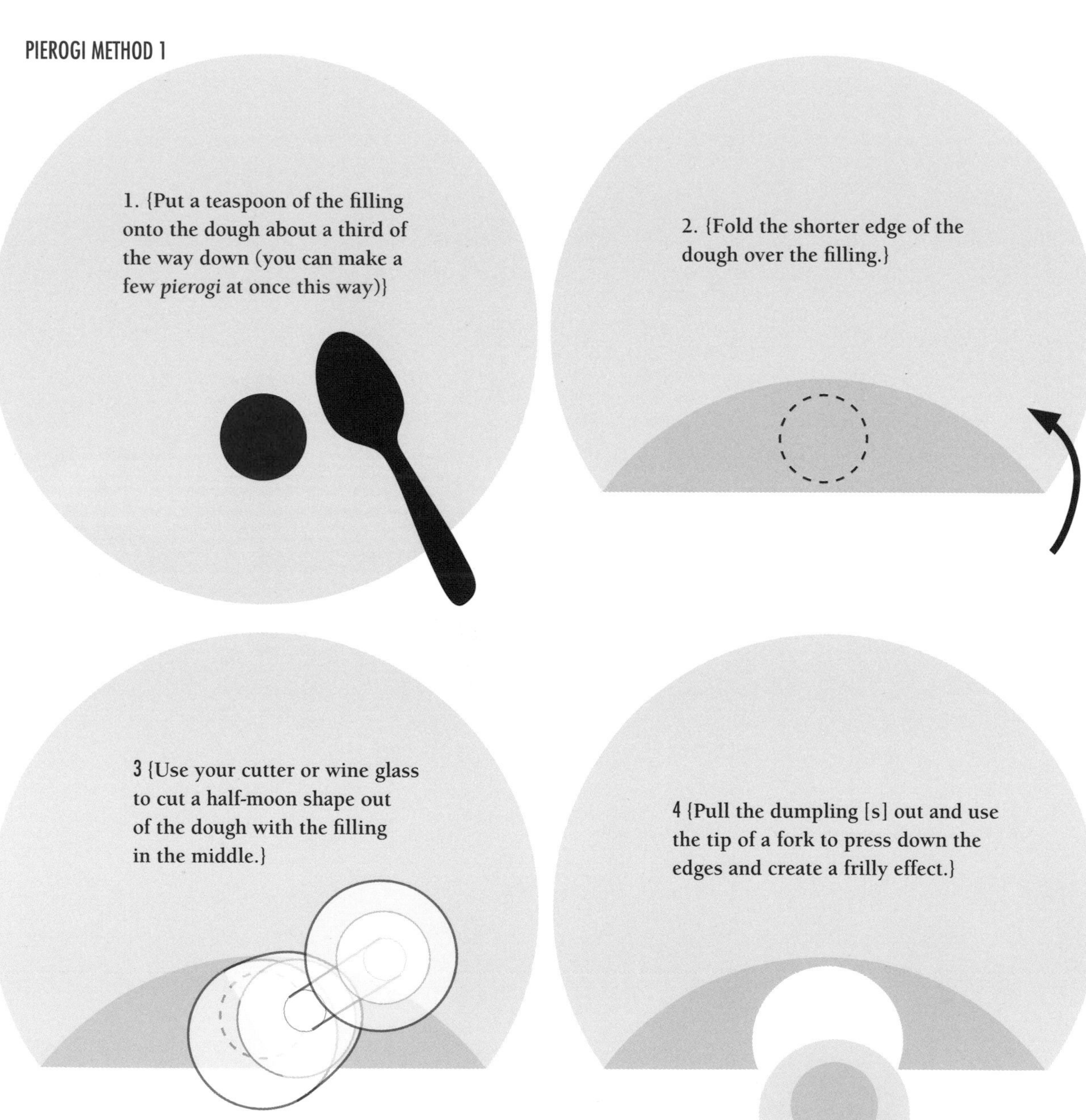

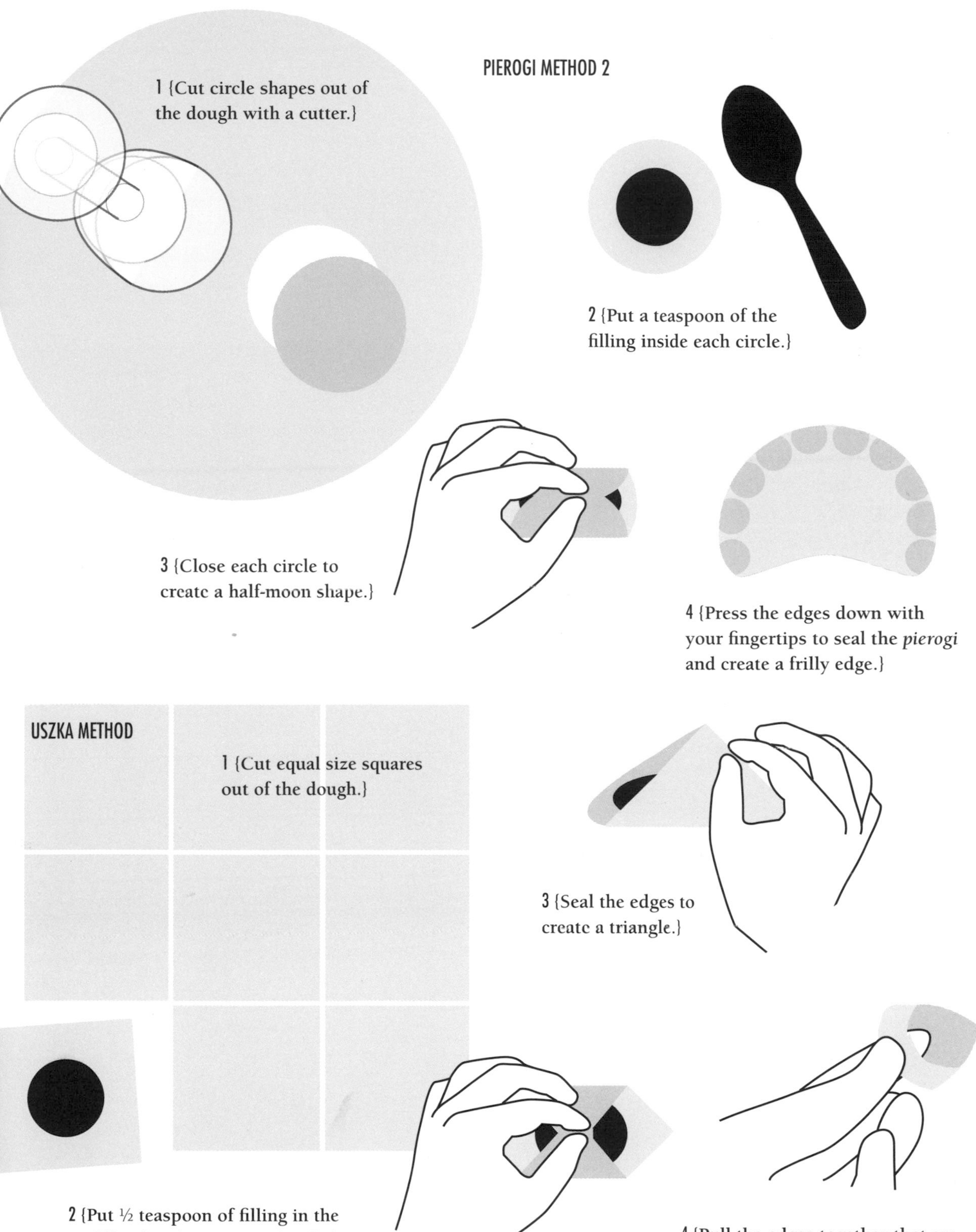

PIEROGI METHOD 2

1 {Cut circle shapes out of the dough with a cutter.}

2 {Put a teaspoon of the filling inside each circle.}

3 {Close each circle to create a half-moon shape.}

4 {Press the edges down with your fingertips to seal the *pierogi* and create a frilly edge.}

USZKA METHOD

1 {Cut equal size squares out of the dough.}

2 {Put ½ teaspoon of filling in the middle of each square and pull the edges together diagonally to close.}

3 {Seal the edges to create a triangle.}

4 {Pull the edges together that are the furthest apart from one another around your little finger.}

Pierogi are one of Poland's signature dishes, their frilly crescent moon shape distinguishes them from other dumplings. It takes a certain amount of skill to get them just right, and I remember my grandma Ziuta repeatedly instructing me to press the sides down more firmly when I sealed them. I never seemed to have the confidence to press down hard enough, and she always worked on the *pierogi* after me, making sure they were firmly sealed. These colourful *pierogi* are my own invention, if you don't have a juicer then you can use water to make the dough, and blend the spinach rather than juicing it and add it to the mixture. **{Serves 4}**

GREEN SPRINGTIME PIEROGI WITH SPINACH, KASZA AND CHEESE

FOR THE DOUGH

300 g (10½ oz/2¼ cups) plain (all-purpose) flour
2 egg yolks
pinch of salt
200 g (7 oz) spinach, juiced (or 3–4 tablespoons spinach juice)
1 tablespoon rapeseed oil
2 tablespoons melted unsalted butter
salt, to taste

FOR THE FILLING

200g (7 oz) spinach
100 g (3½ oz) feta cheese
juice of 1 lemon
½ teaspoon grated nutmeg
100 g (3½ oz) toasted buckwheat groats, cooked
salt and white pepper, to taste

100g (3½ oz) watercress, to serve

To make the dough, combine the flour with the egg yolks, a pinch of salt and some of the spinach juice in a bowl and knead together for about 10 minutes, adding more spinach juice to bring the dough together into a ball that has the consistency of play dough. Add a little oil and butter to make the dough more elastic and continue kneading for another 2 minutes or so. Cover with a damp tea towel and leave to rest for about 20 minutes, if possible.

Meanwhile, chop the spinach for the filling, place in a bowl and cover with boiling water. Leave for a minute or two and then drain thoroughly in a sieve, pressing down with a fork to make sure all the water has drained away. Return to the bowl, add the feta, lemon juice, nutmeg, buckwheat groats and some white pepper.

Roll out your dough as thinly as possible on a floured surface. Use either *pierogi* method (see page 152–153).

Bring a large pan of lightly salted water to the boil and add the rapeseed oil. When it's bubbling drop a few *pierogi* in, 5 or 6 at a time. When they float up to the top give them another 3–4 minutes, then remove from the pan with a slotted spoon. Cook the remaining *pierogi* in the same way.

Serve the *pierogi* with the watercress as a garnish.

{Time: 1 hour}

Even though I'm not the most green-fingered person, I do love growing my own fruit and vegetables. Strawberries are particularly easy and they taste even more delicious when they come from a plant you've nurtured.

In this recipe, I've used beetroot juice to colour the *pierogi* dough – a juicer is ideal for this. As soon as the *pierogi* dough is the correct consistency, stop adding the juice and add the remainder to the water that you cook the *pierogi* in. If you don't have a juicer you could replace the beetroot juice with shop-bought beetroot juice. **{Serves 4}**

PINK SUMMER PIEROGI WITH STRAWBERRY FILLING AND VANILLA CREAM

FOR THE DOUGH

300 g (10½ oz/2¼ cups) plain (all-purpose) flour
2 egg yolks
2 tablespoons unsalted butter
juice of fresh 4 beetroot (beets) or 50–100ml of shop bought beetroot (beet) juice
1 tablespoon rapeseed oil

FOR THE FILLING

125 g (4½ oz/scant 1 cup) strawberries
1 tablespoon caster (superfine) sugar

FOR THE SAUCE

125g g (4½ oz) strawberries
1 tablespoon caster (superfine) sugar

TO SERVE

100 ml (3½ fl oz/scant ½ cup) whipping cream
seeds from 1 vanilla pod (bean) or 1 teaspoon vanilla extract
1 tablespoon icing (confectioners') sugar

Make the dough by combining the flour, egg yolks, butter and half the beetroot juice (only add more if the dough still feels too dry).

Knead the dough for a couple of minutes, then add the oil and continue to knead until it becomes quite elastic – another 7–8 minutes or so. Cover with a damp tea towel and leave to rest for about 20 minutes.

Meanwhile, prepare the strawberries for the filling. Place the strawberries in a bowl and cover with the sugar. Place the strawberries for the sauce in a pan with a tablespoon of sugar and place over a low heat until they have burst and released their juices.

Roll out your dough as thinly as possible on a floured surface. Use either *pierogi* method (see page 152–153) and then stuff your *pierogi* with the raw strawberry mixture

Bring a large pan of lightly salted water and leftover beetroot juice to the boil. When it's bubbling drop a few *pierogi* in, 5 or 6 at a time. When they float to the top give them another 3–4 minutes, then remove from the pan with a slotted spoon. Cook the remaining *pierogi* in the same way.

Meanwhile, whip the cream with the vanilla and icing sugar until fluffy.

Divide the cooked *pierogi* between bowls and serve with the stewed strawberry sauce and the vanilla cream.

{Time: 45 minutes}

'Little hooves' and 'lazy dumplings' look very similar, yet as soon as you taste them their difference becomes obvious. 'Little hooves' are savoury and similar in texture to Italian gnocchi. I have vivid memories of making these in my grandma Ziuta's kitchen, which didn't have any windows, it was dark and small and we would sit there, as if in a bird's nest and make these 'little hooves'. It was our own little world, one with just me and my grandma in it. **{Serves 4}**

'LITTLE HOOVES' WITH CRISPY ONION AND BACON BITS

3 large potatoes, peeled
3–4 tablespoons rapeseed oil
3–4 medium shallots, thinly sliced
4 rashers bacon, finely chopped
1 egg
200 g (7 oz/1½ cups) plain (all-purpose) flour
sea salt and black pepper, to taste

Cook the potatoes in boiling, salted water until they fall apart when you poke them. Drain and mash with a bit of salt until they are perfectly smooth. Tip the mixture onto a flour-dusted work surface to cool down.

Heat the oil in a frying pan (skillet) and fry the shallots and bacon bits over a medium heat for about 5 minutes, or until crispy. Season with salt and pepper.

Make a dent in the middle of your potato mixture and break the egg into it. Add the flour and quickly knead it all together before the egg has a chance to leak and get messy. Roll the mixture into three snake-like cylinders.

Bring a large pan of salted water to a boil. Cut the dough diagonally into 'little hooves' then throw (not too violently as you might burn yourself) into the pan. Cook them in batches as you don't want to overcrowd the pan and end up with a sticky mess. Once they float to the top, give them about 3–4 minutes more, then remove them with a slotted spoon and drain. Repeat until all of them have been cooked.

Add the cooked hooves to the pan of crispy shallots and bacon and fry for a minute or two before serving.

{Time: 35 minutes}

'Lazy' dumplings have a dreamy melt-in-your-mouth texture and an indisputably lovely delicate, sweet flavour. This would normally be made with *twaróg*, a fresh curd cheese that you find everywhere in Poland, but I have replaced it with ricotta as I prefer the milder flavour and creamier texture. **{Serves 4}**

'LAZY' DUMPLINGS WITH SUGARY BROWN BUTTER

Blend the egg yolks with half of the butter until smooth (this may take a little time). Add the ricotta and blend again until completely combined. Beat the egg whites until they form soft peaks and slowly add these to the mixture. Sift in the flour and mix gently to combine. Blend it all together with a pinch of salt.

Bring a large pan of lightly salted water to a boil while you shape the dumplings.

Dust a clean work surface with flour and tip the mixture onto it. Start to knead the mixture into a ball, adding more flour if it feels too sticky. After 5 minutes, separate the mixture into two or three pieces and roll them into long cylinders. Be gentle, as this dough is soft and fragile. Once you've rolled them out, form them into three flattish snake-shapes, making sure they're covered in flour. Be careful with the flour, as you don't want the dumplings to become too dense, but if the mixture is so sticky it is unmanageable then there is not enough flour, so add it in bit by bit, until it's just workable for you.

Chop the snakes into even, diagonal, bite-sized pieces and drop into the boiling water, in batches. Once they float to the top, give them 2–3 minutes more. Remove with a slotted spoon, and transfer them to a plate while you cook the rest.

Make the sauce: melt the remaining butter in a pan. When it is bubbling add the sugar and stir together for a couple of minutes. Add the breadcrumbs and fry until golden, then add the cinnamon.

Add the dumplings to the pan and coat in the delicious mixture. Serve with a dollop of soured cream.

{Time: 40 minutes}

3 eggs, separated
80 g (3 oz/6 tablespoons) salted butter, softened
500 g (1 lb 2 oz/2¼ cups) ricotta
150 g (5 oz/1⅛ cups) plain (all-purpose) flour
pinch of salt
2 tablespoons soft brown sugar
50 g (1¾ oz/⅓ cup) dried breadcrumbs
large pinch of ground cinnamon
soured cream, to serve
cinnamon, to garnish

{Autumnal Potato Knedle with Juicy Plum Filling}

Plums immediately come to my mind when I think of early autumn and these dumplings hold a special place in both my heart and stomach.

This sugary, soft dumpling releases its glorious, sweet-yet-tangy, fragrant juiciness once pierced with a knife. As soon as you smell the sweetness of the cooked plum and see the juices escaping out onto the plate it's very hard to wait before eating them, but wait you must – just for a moment – before you bite into this small piece of heaven as it is too hot for immediate consumption. **{Serves 4}**

AUTUMNAL POTATO KNEDLE WITH JUICY PLUM FILLING

300 g (10½ oz) plums, pitted
100 g (3½ oz/½ cup) brown sugar, plus extra to serve
350 g (12 oz) potatoes, cooked and mashed
125 g (4½ oz/1 cup) plain (all-purpose) flour
1 small egg
pinch of salt
50 g (1¾ oz/ 3½ tablespoons) salted butter
125 g (4 oz/scant 1 cup) dried breadcrumbs

First place the plums in a bowl with half the brown sugar and toss to coat.

Combine the mashed potatoes with the flour, egg and salt in a bowl and knead it with your hands until you create a doughy consistency. Turn out onto a floured surface and roll into a baguette shape. Cut the baguette shape into even slices, and make a little dent in each one. Place a sugary plum in each one, fold the dough over and pinch all the way round to seal them.

Bring a pan of lightly salted water to a boil and place all the dumplings in it. When the dumplings float to the top, cook for a further 4–5 minutes.

While the dumplings are cooking, melt three-quarters of the butter in a frying pan (skillet) and fry the breadcrumbs for a few minutes until golden brown. Drain the dumplings well, then transfer them to the pan of breadcrumbs and fry for a minute or two, until they are coated with the breadcrumbs.

Melt the remaining butter in a separate frying pan and add any leftover plums. Cook for a minute or two, until they release their juices.

Serve the dumplings with the plum sauce on the side, sprinkled with brown sugar.

{Time: 1 hour}

Crispy *pierogi* are not a common dumpling, but they are a great alternative to *uszka* with clear red borscht and also work well with *żurek* (see page 80 and 169). You should eat these on the side of soups, so that they retain their crunchy consistency. Baked *pierogi* require a slightly different dough, similar to that of the famous Russian *kulebiak*, which is just one massive ornately decorated dumpling. **{Serves 4}**

CRISPY-BAKED PIEROGI STUFFED WITH PORK AND PINE NUTS

FOR THE DOUGH

350 g (12 oz/scant 3 cups) plain (all-purpose) flour
150 g (5 oz/1⅔ sticks) salted butter, softened
2 tablespoons rapeseed oil
100 ml (3½ fl oz/scant ½ cup) ice-cold water
beaten egg yolk, to glaze

FOR THE FILLING

200 g (7 oz) minced (ground) pork
50 g (1¾ oz/½ cup) pine nuts, toasted
1 egg
salt and white pepper, to taste

Tip the flour into a bowl and add the butter and oil. Work into the flour using your hands for a few minutes, then add the ice-cold water, a little at a time. Start kneading until it comes together into a smooth ball. Knead for a further 3–4 minutes then place in a plastic food bag in the fridge for at least 30 minutes.

Preheat the oven to 200°C (400°F/gas 6) and lightly grease a baking tray.

To make the filling, combine the pork mince, pine nuts, egg and seasoning together in a bowl, using your hands.

Roll out your dough as thinly as possible on a floured surface. Use either *pierogi* method (see page 152–153), filling them with the pork and pine nut mixture.

Place the *pierogi* on the baking tray and brush with a beaten egg yolk to glaze. Bake in the oven for 30 minutes.

{Time: 1 hour, plus resting time}

The Polish dumpling has become a symbol of our entire cuisine, and I must concede that there appears to be a dumpling for every occasion in this country. This is the Christmas dumpling. We eat these 'little ears' in a clear borscht. You can buy this borscht from a Polish shop or make it yourself (see page 72). **{Serves 4}**

USZKA – WILD MUSHROOM AND SAUERKRAUT 'LITTLE EARS'

FOR THE DOUGH

400 g (14 oz/3¼ cups) plain (all-purpose) flour
2 egg yolks
2 tablespoons unsalted butter, melted
pinch of salt
125–150 ml (4–5 fl oz/½–⅔ cup) warm water
splash of rapeseed oil

FOR THE FILLING

10–20 dried mushrooms, chopped (about 150 g/5 oz)
150 g (5 oz) sauerkraut (see page 251), drained
1 bay leaf
¼ teaspoon allspice berries
splash of wine (red or white), optional
1 tablespoon unsalted butter
2 small onions or 1 large one, finely chopped
salt and white pepper, to taste

First make the filling. Rinse the dried mushrooms under cold water and soak them in boiling water for 2 hours, preferably, overnight. Place the rehydrated mushrooms in a pan with about 2.5 cm (1 in) of water over the top and cook over a medium heat for about 45 minutes. Add the sauerkraut, bay leaf and allspice and simmer for a further 45 minutes. Add a splash of wine if the mixture gets too dry at any time, but don't overdo it – there should not be any surplus liquid near the end.

Meanwhile, make the dough. Place the flour, egg yolks, butter and salt in a large bowl. Add the warm water, a little at a time, and mix until the dough comes together. Knead it for about 20 minutes until soft and smooth. Cover the bowl with a damp tea towel and leave to rest at room temperature for a further 20 minutes. (This step is not absolutely necessary but it does increase its elasticity, so is worth doing while your mushroom and sauerkraut mixture cooks.)

To finish the filling, melt the butter in a frying pan (skillet) and fry the onion over a medium heat for about 5 minutes, or until golden.

Remove the bay leaf from the sauerkraut and mushroom pan and blend the filling to a rough paste in a food processor, then add it to the onion and fry for just 5 minutes, stirring together until combined. Allow the filling to cool while you roll the dough out on a floured surface, as thin as you can get it. Follow the *uszka* diagram (see page 153) to shape the 'little ears'.

Bring a pan of salted water to a boil, then reduce to a simmer. Drop the *uszka* gently into the water. Once they float to the top, cook for a further 3 minutes before removing with a slotted spoon.

Serve in a bowl of borscht (see page 71) or clear vegetarian borscht (see page 72).

{Time: 2 hours, plus soaking, resting and cooling time}

Vilnius in Lithuania is a mythical place, which lives on only in the hearts of the people who inhabited it before World War II. It was talked about as a slice of heaven with green pastures and orchards that were abundant in fruit. My grandma Halinka, frequently described it as a place where everyone was kind, and looked out for one another.

Poland and Lithuania have been like brothers throughout history, at times joined at the hip and at other times feuding. Therefore, Lithuanian cuisine has understandably had an impact on Polish cuisine. These dumplings are based on a Vilnius recipe that my grandma often reminisced about, this my interpretation, an ode to lost lands and times. **{Serves 4}**

LITHUANIAN-STYLE BEEF AND LAMB PYZY

- 5 large potatoes, peeled and cut into chunks
- rapeseed oil, for frying
- 100 g (3½ oz) minced (ground) lamb
- 100 g (3½ oz) minced (ground) beef
- ¼ teaspoon ground cinnamon
- 1 shallot, finely chopped
- 1 egg
- 2 tablespoons plain (all-purpose) flour
- salt and white pepper, to taste

Cook the potatoes in boiling, salted water until completely soft. Drain, then mash (without adding any butter) until smooth. Allow to cool.

Meanwhile, heat a little rapeseed oil in a large frying pan (skillet) and fry the lamb and beef over a medium heat, using a fork to mash them together. After about 5 minutes add the cinnamon and continue to mash while frying. Season with salt and pepper and allow to cool slightly.

In a separate pan, fry the chopped shallot in a little oil until crispy. Season with salt and pepper and set aside.

Add the egg and flour to the cooled mashed potatoes and squeeze it all together with your hands. Season with salt and pepper. You need to make sure the potato dough sticks together well, neither too sticky nor too hard.

Take a spoonful of the dough and form it into a flat pancake shape. Fill with a tablespoon of the meat mixture, seal the edges to make an oblong shape. Repeat with the remaining dough and filling, this should make about twelve.

Bring a large pan of salted water to a boil. Carefully lower the *pyzy* into the water one at a time, then reduce the heat right down and simmer, covered, for about 5 minutes.

Remove the *pyzy* with a slotted spoon and transfer them to the pan of crispy shallots. Roll them around in the oily onions and their juice, before serving.

{Time: 50 minutes, plus cooling time}

These are my favourite winter *pierogi* – although *knedle* are still my year-round favourites. This is a traditional filling from the area where I come from, although confusingly we call their filling 'Russian'.

You can replace the *twaróg* in this recipe with other mild white cheese, ricotta works very well. **{Serves 2}**

PIEROGI RUSKIE – MY FAVOURITE WINTER DUMPLINGS

Make the dough by combining the flour with the egg yolks, melted butter, salt and enough of the warm water to bring the mixture together in a medium bowl. Knead the mixture until it is smooth (10 minutes should suffice), adding more water if you need it. Cover with a damp tea towel (dish towel) and allow to rest for 20 minutes.

Chop your onions very finely and fry them in 1 tablespoon of butter. Combine the *twaróg* (or other soft cheese) with half of the fried onions, diced cooked potato and season to taste with salt and pepper (some cheeses are saltier than others so it's important to season to taste).

Roll out your dough as thinly as possible on a floured surface. Use either *pierogi* method (see page 152–53), filling them with the potato and cheese mixture. Have some water on standby to help you seal the edges if the dough is a little bit too dry to stick together.

Bring a large pan of salted water to a boil and carefully lower the *pierogi* into the water (you'll need to cook these in two batches). As soon as the *pierogi* float to the top, after about 4–5 minutes, leave them to cook for a further 2–3 minutes. Remove from the pan with a slotted spoon and transfer to the frying pan of buttery onions.

Fry the *pierogi* for a minute or two, making sure they are all covered in the buttery onion mixture. Serve immediately.

{Time: 45 minutes}

FOR THE DOUGH

300 g (10½ oz/2½ cups) plain (all-purpose) flour
2 egg yolks
2 tablespoons melted unsalted butter
large pinch of salt
100 ml (3½ fl oz/scant ½ cup) warm water (from a boiled kettle)

FOR THE FILLING

2 onions
2 tablespoons salted butter
150 g (5 oz) *twaróg* or other soft cheese
1 potato, peeled, cooked and diced
salt and white pepper, to taste

PARTY FOOD
(ZAKĄSKI)

Zakąski ('za-kon-ski') is the Polish word for party food – or snacks to be eaten while drinking vodka. Except that snacks is a deceptive word, considering the time and care we use to prepare these *hors d'oeuvres*. In Tsarist Russia, they were called *zakuski* and would be eaten standing up in a less formal setting, such as a library. The words *zakąska* suggests a little morsel of food, a small bite of something, however, it is usually more substantial than that. In Poland, it is unheard of to be a guest in someone's home and to leave feeling hungry. You should always have a few dishes prepared that you can rustle up in case unexpected guests appear, because when they do, it's celebration time!

That's why I call these dishes party food, because this is the spirit that they are always eaten in. *Zakąski* are essentially the Eastern European equivalent of tapas in Spain or meze in the Middle East, although they were invented for drinking solely with vodka – i.e. recipes which can stand up to a few shots of the strong stuff.

"... You don't pour it, our mother vodka, into any old glass... and don't drink it straight off, but first sniff it, rub your hands, look up at the ceiling nonchalantly, then, without hurrying, raise that little glass to your lips and straight away sparks travel from your stomach through your whole body... and the very minute you've drunk it you must take a bite".

{*The Siren*, Anton Chekhov}

My father believes that proper, authentic *zakąski* must contain some kind of fat to neutralise the vodka. However, things have changed a little since his day and vodka is no longer obligatory. It all depends on the time of day and the circumstances; beer, wine or cocktails all go well with *zakąski*, although if it is a big celebration then shots are inevitable. The concept is that food and drink always go hand in hand. It should be a Polish proverb that if you do a shot of vodka you always have to have something to swallow it down with.

The *zakąski* dishes vary depending on region, the time of year and the time of day. In some parts of Poland there will always be pâté and pickles, while in other areas you will get many varieties of fish. In most parts of Russia and many Slavic States (which at various times in history belonged to either Poland or Russia) you would always have caviar and blinis, even if it is just vegetable caviar. *Zakąski* will always combine the ingredients that the seasons bring and the earth and waters provide to each region of Poland.

"Although it is a country quite wooded, [it] abounds in… bread and meat, fish and honey… and although it is surrounded by so many Christian and pagan peoples and repeatedly assaulted… [it is] a country where the air is healthy, the earth fertile, the woods flowing with honey and the waters full of fish."
{Gallus Anonymus, 12th Century}

The main point of *zakąski* is that it is food designed for sharing. I grew up surrounded by a large extended family, and even though you couldn't find much food in shops during those grey, Communist days, a huge amount of time and care was spent on preparing, cooking and eating food. Families and neighbours were close, because they needed one another to survive. Everyone would bring something new to the table and together we would prepare incredible feasts from moderate means (all home-grown and reared). Despite the difficult political climate of those times – or perhaps as a result of it – there was always an excuse for a party.

"The main principle of the Polish way of life is hospitality: a Pole does not like eating alone… when someone slaughters a pig, catches some fish or has some early vegetables, he soon invites company… his hospitality is reciprocated with equal politeness".
{Łukasz Gołembiowski, 18th Century}

As you eat *zakąski*, I invite you to find something to celebrate and to be grateful for. If you are doing shots, then this is actually obligatory, as with each shot you must make a short toast. If you chose this traditional approach to *zakąski* – washed down with plenty of vodka, then serve the vodka ice-cold. Remember to make a toast, drink it on the in-breath and follow up with a bite of food immediately after your sip or shot. Breathe out as the food enters your mouth. The toast can be anything from the simple *na zdrowie* (to health), to a more elaborate exclamation of gratitude.

So, you Polish people have Tatar genes on you!

Tartare is named after the nomadic Tatar horse-backed clan from the East, who rampaged the Polish lands, mincing horse meat under their saddles as they rode.

Make sure you use a respected butcher and request the best meat they have. You can also ask your butcher to mince the meat for you, but I prefer to chop it myself as finely as I can get it, then pulse it a couple of times in a food processor, as this adds more texture. **{Serves 1}**

From Mongolia

GENGHIS KHAN'S BEEF TARTARE WITH QUAIL'S EGG

- 100 g (3½ oz) finely chopped or minced organic beef fillet (tenderloin) steak
- 1 shallot, finely chopped
- 1 gherkin, finely chopped
- ½ teaspoon Sarepska or Dijon mustard
- ¼ teaspoon white pepper
- salt, to taste
- 1 quail's egg

Put the finely chopped minced (ground) meat in a bowl and, using your hands, blend it with all the other ingredients, except the quail's egg, adding salt and pepper as you mix it all together – tasting and adjusting the seasoning as you go. When it is to your taste, put it into a small bowl that has been rinsed in cold water, then chill in the fridge for half an hour to set it.

When ready to serve, tip the bowl upside down onto a serving plate and make a tiny indentation in the middle of the domed tartare. Carefully wash the outside of the quail's egg and then break it into the tartare. Serve immediately.

{Time: 10 minutes, plus chilling time}

Curing fish in vodka is a great way of enjoying two of Poland's favourite ingredients, vodka and fish. Ask your fishmonger to slice the tuna as thinly as possible or do it yourself with a very sharp knife.

The east of Poland is home to the last herd of European bison. They live in Białowieża National Park, in ancient woodland. As a nation we have a natural affiliation to these dark, exotic creatures who have shared our land with us for so long. It's why Poland's favourite vodka is called Bison Grass vodka, which has been flavoured with a bitter herb called bison grass, and is now available worldwide. **{Serves 2}**

TUNA CURED IN BISON GRASS VODKA

1 fresh tuna steak, about 120 g (4 oz), finely sliced
½ cucumber, peeled and cut into paper-thin slices
1 tablespoon fresh chives, finely chopped
25 ml (1 fl oz/2 tablespoons) Bison Grass vodka
juice of 1 lemon
1 tablespoon apple juice
pinch of sea salt
large pinch of white pepper

Place the tuna, cucumber slices and half the chives in a shallow bowl (reserve a couple of cucumber slices to garnish).

Combine the vodka, lemon juice, apple juice and salt and pepper in a pestle and mortar and grind together until the salt has completely dissolved. Pour over the fish and cucumber and gently stir to combine all the ingredients.

Divide between two martini glasses and chill in the fridge for at least 30 minutes before serving. Serve with each glass with a slice of cucumber on the rim and dress with the remaining chives.

{Time: 5 minutes, plus chilling time}

Hunting was a national pastime in Poland for hundreds of years. Now it takes place mainly in the more rugged mountain regions, such as the Karpaty Mountains or in the less frequented forests such as those that border with Belarus. Nevertheless, our taste for game remains strong.

Buckwheat honey, or *miód gryczany,* has a very strong, piney flavour; if you find yourself in a Polish food shop I would recommend buying some as you won't find it anywhere else. If you can't find this particular honey, then Australian eucalyptus honey is a good alternative, or any other honey that is treacle-coloured and full of flavour – as it needs to offset the gamey quail meat. **{Serves 5}**

QUAILS WITH BUCKWHEAT HONEY AND CUMIN

5 teaspoons strong-flavoured honey
5 teaspoons olive oil
2 teaspoons ground cumin
5 quails
1 orange, cut into wedges
sea salt and black pepper, to taste

Mix together the honey, olive oil, cumin and some salt and pepper to make a marinade and then massage into the birds.

Put an orange wedge inside each bird's bottom, arrange them in a roasting tray and set aside for at least 30 minutes. Preheat the oven to 150°C (300°F/gas 2).

Cover the roasting tray with foil and roast the birds for about 20 minutes. Increase the oven temperature to 200°C (400°F/gas 6), remove the foil and cook the quails for a further 5 minutes to crisp up the skin.

Remove the quails from the oven, cover with the foil once again and allow to rest for 10 minutes before serving.

{Time: 35 minutes, plus resting time}

"TYLKO TRUDNY STRZAŁ JEST PIĘKNYM STRZAŁEM."

"Only a difficult shot, is a beautiful shot."
{Polish proverb}

These fluffy, white *babkas* look beautiful floating on top of a red sea of peppers. This dish hails from the tallest and most imposing Tartra Mountains that Poland shares with Slovenia. The mountain folk here have their own specific culture, which they fiercely preserve. It is not uncommon to see them wearing their traditional costumes to church on Sunday. They make beautiful engraved, wooden objects and have their own music and dialect. This recipe is dedicated to them. **{Serves 6}**

CUMIN BABKAS ON A SEA OF MARINATED RED PEPPERS

FOR THE MARINATED (BELL) PEPPERS

2 red (bell) peppers, sliced
1 tablespoon olive oil
1 tablespoon white wine vinegar
1 tablespoon fresh thyme
1 bay leaf
salt and black pepper, to taste

FOR THE BABKAS

250 g (9 oz/generous 1 cup) ricotta
2 eggs, separated
½ teaspoon white wine vinegar
¼ teaspoon ground cumin
larch pinch of sea salt

First prepare the marinated peppers. Rub the red peppers with some olive oil and a little salt and place under a hot grill (broiler) for about 7 minutes, turning them regularly so that they are slightly charred on all sides.

Once they've cooled down, slice them, discarding the core and seeds, and place them in a small bowl. Pour over enough white wine vinegar to cover, add the fresh thyme, bay leaf and some freshly ground black pepper. Leave to marinate for at least 1 hour, ideally overnight.

When you are ready to make the *babkas*, preheat the oven to 150°C (300°F/gas 2) and lightly grease six silicone cupcake moulds. Blend the ricotta thoroughly with the egg yolks. Beat the egg whites in a separate bowl with the vinegar, until they form soft peaks, and fold into the ricotta mixture. Stir in the cumin and salt and pour into the greased silicone moulds.

Bake in the oven for about 30 minutes, or until golden. Serve the *babkas* on top of the marinated red peppers.

{Time: 45 minutes, plus marinating time}

Early autumn is the time for our favourite pastime: mushroom picking. Chanterelles and other wild mushrooms are sold in large wooden crates by the roadside throughout the autumn months in Poland.

We serve each *placek* (potato cake) with a small dollop of flavoursome topping, which needs to be rich and creamy. You can keep the *placki* warm in the oven, while you prepare the sauce, so there's no need to rush. Just cover them with foil and keep the heat low to prevent them from drying out. **{Serves 4}**

POTATO PLACKI WITH CREAMY CHANTERELLES

2 large potatoes, peeled
½ onion
1 tablespoon plain (all-purpose) flour
1 egg
rapeseed oil, for frying
25g salted butter
200 g (7 oz) chanterelles
2 garlic cloves, crushed
1 teaspoon dried thyme
1 tablespoon fresh thyme leaves
200 ml (7 fl oz/scant 1 cup) single (light) cream
salt and white pepper, to taste

Finely grate the potatoes and onion into a bowl, so that they turn to mush. Pour out any excess water. Mix together to combine and then sift in the flour and add the egg. Season well with salt and pepper and mix again until fully combined.

Heat a little oil in a large, heavy-based frying pan (skillet) over a medium heat. When the oil is hot enough (a small spoonful of the mixture should sizzle as soon as it hits the pan), add spoonfuls of the mixture to the pan – each *placek* should be about 10–12 cm (4–5 in) in diameter. Fry for about 15 minutes, turning halfway through cooking, until golden brown on both sides. Keep the *placki* warm in a low heat oven while you repeat the process for the remaining mixture.

Melt the butter in a separate, large pan over a medium heat and add the mushrooms. Cook for about 15 minutes, until browned, stirring occasionally. Add the garlic, dried and fresh thyme and plenty of salt and pepper. Fry for a couple of minutes longer, before adding the cream. Turn the heat down and simmer for 7–10 minutes to allow the sauce to thicken and reduce, stirring often.

Serve the *placki* with a dollop of the sauce on top.

{Time: 1 hour}

In Poland we like to combine salty herrings with something sweet – an apple, some prunes or a sprinkle of cinnamon all work very well to balance the saltiness. In my family, this dish is a celebration staple – whether Christmas Eve, Easter or a wedding, these herrings are usually on the table. They are delicious eaten with rye bread or stuffed into bagels. **{Serves 5}**

RUSTIC HERRINGS WITH OLIVE OIL AND CINNAMON

- 250 g (9 oz) herrings preserved in oil, drained
- 1 shallot, very finely chopped
- 300 ml (10 fl oz/1¼ cups) mild olive oil to cover
- ¼ teaspoon white pepper
- ¼ teaspoon ground cinnamon

Chop the herrings into bite-sized pieces and place in a shallow bowl. Scatter over the finely chopped shallot and then pour over the olive oil. Stir in the white pepper and cinnamon. (You won't need any salt as the herrings are already quite salty.)

For best results chill in the fridge overnight before serving on rye bread or stuffed into bagels for lunch. Eat within 3 days.

{Time: 5 minutes, plus chilling time}

My first ever memory of nettles was watching my grandma Halinka beating her legs with them in the Łazienki Gardens in Warsaw, to 'improve her circulation'. Ever since, I have remained fascinated by this seemingly dangerous plant that hides so many beneficial qualities behind its prickly façade.

Tough times throughout Poland's history have instilled a self-reliance in the heart of every Pole, and now, even though there is no need for it, we still love to forage. It's the familiar feeling of being close to the earth and knowing exactly where the food you eat comes from. **{Serves 5}**

NETTLE LEAVES IN BEER BATTER WITH HONEY MUSTARD DIP

100 g (3½ oz/generous ¾ cup) chickpea (gram) flour, sifted
50 ml (2 fl oz/scant ¼ cup) sparkling water
100 ml (3½ fl oz/scant ½ cup) beer
¼ teaspoon celery salt
1 tablespoon honey
1 tablespoon Sarepska or Dijon mustard
1 tablespoon olive oil
1 tablespoon lemon juice
15 nettle leaves
rapeseed oil, for frying

For the batter, sift the chickpea flour into a large bowl and whisk in the sparkling water. Once you have a smooth batter start adding the beer and keep whisking until the batter is the consistency of double (heavy) cream. Whisk in the celery salt and set aside.

Whisk together the honey, mustard, olive oil and lemon juice to make the dip. Set aside.

Soak the nettles in the batter for about 5 minutes. Meanwhile, pour about 2.5 cm (1 in) of rapeseed oil into a frying pan (skillet) and place over a medium heat. When the oil is hot (a drop of batter should sizzle as soon as it hits the oil) transfer the nettles to the hot oil and fry in batches for 30–45 seconds on each side. As the oil gets hotter they will need less time to brown.

Drain on kitchen paper and serve with the honey mustard dip.

{Time: 15 minutes}

These herrings are as popular in Russia as they are in Poland. In Russia this dish would be known as *pod shuboy,* which translates as 'under a fur coat', referring to the fact that in this recipe the herrings lie snug underneath all the other ingredients. In Poland, we know this dish as *śledzie pod pierzynką*, meaning 'under a duvet'.

The most memorable time I ate this dish was in the Liternaturnoye Café in St Petersburg, where Pushkin had his final glass of water or lemonade – no one is sure – before being mortally wounded in a duel over his love, the beautiful and flirtatious Natalia. **{Serves 5}**

SAINT PETERSBURG-STYLE HERRINGS

2 red beetroot (beet)
1 large potato
150 ml (5 fl oz/2/3 cup) mayonnaise
150 ml (5 fl oz/2/3 cup) soured cream
250 g (9 oz) herring fillets preserved in oil, drained and chopped
1 red onion, finely chopped
2 carrots, grated
1 medium apple, grated
4 hard-boiled eggs, chopped
1 tablespoon chopped fresh dill
salt and white pepper, to taste

Cook the beetroot and potato with the skins on until tender when pierced with a knife. Allow to cool, then peel. Grate the beetroot and thinly slice the potato.

Combine the mayonnaise and soured cream in a bowl. Season to taste.

Arrange the herrings in a single layer in the base of a shallow bowl or plate. Scatter the chopped onion over the top, then add a layer of sliced potato and spoon over half the mayonnaise and soured cream mixture. Add a layer of grated beetroot, the grated carrot and then the apple. Finally, add the chopped egg, the remaining mayonnaise and soured cream. Scatter over the dill. The salad should now look like a colourful cake. Place in the fridge for a couple of hours to chill.

Cut into squares or slices to serve, making sure each guest gets a bit of each layer.

{Time: 45 minutes, plus chilling time}

I have to admit at family get-togethers in Poland I have to stop myself from reaching for this dish first, because I know that when I start to eat it I can't stop and end up feeling too full for any other dishes.

You could use any white fish in this recipe, I prefer Wild Alaska pollock, cod or haddock (line-caught Icelandic cod and haddock are the best).

{Serves 5}

POLLOCK IN SWEET AND AROMATIC RED SAUCE

2–3 tablespoons rapeseed oil
1 onion, finely chopped
3 carrots, grated
½ celeriac (celery root), grated
1 parsnip, grated
1 tablespoon salted butter
250 g (9 oz) pollock fillet, cut into large chunks
plain (all-purpose) flour for coating
100 ml (3½ fl oz/⅔ cup) tomato purée (paste)
1 teaspoon paprika
1 teaspoon caster (superfine) sugar
1 tablespoon lemon juice
1 teaspoon Sarepska or Dijon mustard
salt and pepper (both white and black varieties), to taste

Heat the oil in a pan over a low heat and add all the vegetables. Cover and sweat for about 30 minutes, until softened but not browned.

While the vegetables are cooking melt the butter in a separate frying pan (skillet) over a medium heat. Dust the fish pieces in a little flour and fry in the butter for about 4–5 minutes on each side, turning once, or until golden on both sides. Remove from the pan and set aside to cool.

Add the tomato purée, paprika, sugar, lemon juice, mustard and seasoning to the vegetable pan and simmer together for 15 minutes. Taste and adjust the seasoning, until you are happy with the flavour.

Transfer the fish to a serving dish and cover with the sauce. This dish is served cold, so allow it to cool and then chill in the fridge until ready to serve.

{Time: 45 minutes}

Making blinis is a bit of a ritual: it's simple but not quick, so only embark on making them when you have time to really enjoy the process. If you do get your hands on some caviar (black or red), then serve the blinis with a teaspoon of it, a little dollop of soured cream and a sprinkle of dill or parsley. While black caviar is considered the premium kind, I have always thought that blinis taste best with the plumper, red salmon roe (which my Russian grandfather used to love) or this silky aubergine 'caviar'. **{Serves 5}**

BUCKWHEAT BLINIS WITH AUBERGINE CAVIAR

FOR THE AUBERGINE (EGGPLANT) CAVIAR

4 aubergines (eggplants)
3 garlic cloves, unpeeled
juice of 2 lemons
100ml (3½ fl oz/scant ½ cup) extra-virgin olive oil
handful of finely chopped flat-leaf parsley
salt and white pepper, to taste

FOR THE BUCKWHEAT BLINIS

750 ml (1¼ pints/3 cups) full-fat milk
20 g (¾ oz) fresh yeast
2 teaspoons caster (superfine) sugar
200 g (7 oz/scant 1⅔ cups) plain (all-purpose) flour
2 eggs, separated
200 g (7 oz/scant 1⅔ cups) buckwheat flour
300 g (10½ oz/1¼ cups) melted unsalted butter
2 pinches of salt
rapeseed oil, for frying

TO SERVE

soured cream
chopped fresh dill or parsley

Using kitchen tongs, hold the aubergines over the flame on your hob, turning, until they are soft and charred. Repeat with the garlic cloves. Allow to cool, then peel. Add to a food processor or blender along with the lemon juice and blitz until smooth. Transfer to a bowl and gradually whisk in the oil, until you get a fluffy consistency. Season to taste and stir in the parsley. Chill in the fridge until needed.

To make the blinis, gently heat 175 ml (6 fl oz/¾ cup) of the milk until tepid and then stir in the yeast and sugar. Sift the plain flour into a large bowl and pour in the milk and yeast. Mix well until you have a smooth batter, then set aside in a warm place to rise for 20 minutes. Meanwhile, whisk the egg whites until stiff peaks form.

Now take the bowl with the flour-yeast-milk mixture. Sift in the buckwheat flour and add the remaining milk. Beat with a wooden spoon until well combined and it reaches the consistency of double (heavy) cream. After a few minutes start adding the egg yolks, beaten egg whites, melted butter and salt. Return the bowl to a warm place for another 20 minutes, until the batter has increased in size.

Preheat the oven to its lowest setting so you can keep the blinis warm. Add a little rapeseed oil to a non-stick frying pan (skillet) and place over a medium heat. Start frying the blinis: add about 1 tablespoon of batter to the pan for each blini (they should be about 5 mm/¼ in thick and 8 cm/3 in across). Fry them quickly for about 1 minute on each side and transfer to the oven to keep warm while you cook the rest. Serve as soon as possible with soured cream, topped with the aubergine caviar and some chopped dill.

{Time: 50 minutes, plus rising time}

{Mama's Gherkins with Horseradish and Oak Leaves}

For my mama's gherkins you will need a few unusual materials; a leaf from an oak tree, some horseradish leaves and a big, flat stone that fits into the container. Both leaves are available in the wild and in domestic gardens, but make sure you know what you are looking for before you start foraging.

The gherkins need to be packed tightly, so you need to have plenty of them and a container in which they fit snugly, then place the heavy stone (wrapped in a plastic bag) on top, to press them down. You'll need special gherkin cucumbers for this – they are much smaller than the usual British cucumbers and have a rougher skin. They are often available in Turkish and Polish shops. **{Makes a 2 litre jar (3½ pints/8 cups)}**

MAMA'S GHERKINS WITH HORSERADISH AND OAK LEAVES {see page 192}

- 20–30 small cucumbers
- 1 whole garlic bulb, cloves peeled
- large handful of fresh dill that has flowered
- 1–2 oak tree leaves
- 2–3 horseradish leaves
- 2 tablespoons salt per 1 litre (2 pint/4¼ cups) water

Place the cucumbers, garlic cloves, dill, oak leaves and horseradish leaves in a large ceramic or glass container.

Bring a large pan of water to the boil and add the salt. We used 2 litres (3½ pints/8 cups) of water for about 20 little cucumbers. Allow the water to cool slightly (about 15 minutes) before pouring it into your container. Make sure everything is submerged under the water. Place your large stone in a plastic food bag and place in the container, to weigh down the contents.

Normally, you would leave these for about 48 hours, but you can try them after 24 hours, depending on how pickled you like yours. Once they're to your taste, transfer the cucumbers and the garlic to a sterilised jar, topping up with the pickling brine.

You can either eat the gherkins immediately or seal the jar and store in a cool, dry place for a couple of months. Once opened, eat within 2 weeks.

{Time: 30 minutes, plus 3–5 days pickling time}

Klopsiki, or meatballs, are common in Poland, often eaten with *kasza* and gherkins for dinner, yet I prefer them perched on top of courgette islands and decorated with dill flowers as a warm *zakąska*. This makes them much lighter and infinitely prettier. You need a big, round courgettes for this, and you can also add slices of yellow squash for colour. **{Serves 8–10}**

PORK KLOPSIKI ON COURGETTE ISLANDS {see page 197}

For the meatballs, melt the butter in a lidded frying pan (skillet) over a low-medium heat and add the onion. Cook for 5 minutes with the lid on, then remove lid and cook for a further 5 minutes.

Put the pork mince in a bowl with the breadcrumbs, marjoram and fried onion. Season well and mix with your hands, then divide and roll into 8–12 balls, of about 5 cm (2 in) in diameter.

To make the sauce, heat the olive oil in a pan and fry the onion and carrot over a medium heat for about 5 minutes, stirring occasionally. Add the tomatoes, cover the pan and reduce the heat. Cook for 10 minutes, until the tomatoes have disintegrated. Stir in the tomato purée, red wine and dill, cover and cook for a further 10 minutes. Add the sugar and season to taste. Add the ground linseeds and increase the heat. As soon as the sauce comes to a boil, remove from the heat and allow to cool before transferring to a food processor and blending to a paste. Return to the pan and set to one side.

In a separate pan, fry the meatballs in the rapeseed oil over a medium heat for 3 minutes each side, until evenly golden. Meanwhile, bring the sauce to a simmer. Add the meatballs to the sauce and cook them for 15–20 minutes. While the meatballs are cooking, slice the courgette (or squash) into 1 cm (½ in) slices and place a griddle pan over a medium heat. Drizzle the courgette slices with olive oil, season and griddle until slightly charred.

To create the island, place a bit of tomato sauce on the plate, then a courgette slice, a tablespoon of tomato sauce, another slice of courgette and repeat until you have a tower of about four or five slices. Top each tower with a meatball and a sprinkling of dill flowers on the top.

{Time: 1 hour 10 minutes}

FOR THE MEATBALLS

1 tablespoon salted butter
1 small onion, finely chopped
400 g (14 oz) minced (ground) pork
2 tablespoons fine breadcrumbs
2 tablespoons dried marjoram
salt and white pepper
4 tablespoons rapeseed oil, for frying

FOR THE SAUCE

2 tablespoons mild olive oil
1 small onion, roughly chopped
1 carrot, roughly grated
500 g (1 lb 2 oz) fresh tomatoes, skinned and chopped
1 tablespoon tomato purée (paste)
350 ml (12 fl oz/1½ cups) red wine
large bunch of dill, chopped, plus dill flowers to garnish, (optional)
1 teaspoon caster (superfine) sugar
1 tablespoon ground linseeds (flaxseeds)
salt and white pepper, to taste

2–3 round courgettes (zucchini) or squash
olive oil, for drizzling
salt and black pepper, to taste

{Pork Klopsiki on Courgette Islands}

This recipe has been in my family for many years, and my uncle Kazik passed it down to me. He is a labourer by day and food lover by night – he typifies our people, who are all culinary experts in their own homes. This simple sweet and savoury pâté goes particularly well with my Mama's pickled gherkins (see page 194). **{Serves 10–12}**

UNCLE KAZIK'S THREE-MEAT PÂTÉ WITH PRUNES

vegetable oil, for frying
250 g (9 oz) streaky (lean) bacon or pancetta
250 g (9 oz) chicken breast
250 g (9 oz) pork belly
350 g (12 oz) braising beef
2 small onions
large handful of dried wild mushrooms, soaked in boiling water for 10 minutes
3 bay leaves
1 tablespoon dried marjoram
½ teaspoon dried pimento berries
½ teaspoon whole black peppercorns
250 g (9 oz) pork liver (or use any other liver)
1 stale white bread roll
handful of pitted prunes
3 eggs
2 teaspoons grated nutmeg
1 teaspoon dried breadcrumbs
1 tablespoon fine (sea) salt or to taste

Heat a tablespoon of vegetable oil in a large frying pan (skillet) and fry the bacon, chicken, pork belly and beef, in batches, until seared on all sides, adding more oil to the pan as necessary. Transfer each batch of seared meat to a large pan along with the oil it's been fried in.

Add the onions, soaked wild mushrooms, bay leaves, marjoram, pimento berries and peppercorns and enough water to cover the meat. Cover with a lid and bring to a simmer, then reduce the heat and cook for 1¾ hours. Add the liver and cook for a further 10–15 minutes. Finally, add the stale bread, remove from the heat and allow to cool for at least 3 hours, preferably overnight.

The following day, transfer the meat, onions, mushrooms, pimento berries and peppercorns (discard the bay leaves) into a food processor and blitz along with the prunes until you get a smooth-ish consistency. Put it into a large bowl and add the cooking liquid (this will give the pâté moisture).

Now, break in the eggs, roll up your sleeves and squish the mixture between your hands until it's all completely smooth. Add the salt and nutmeg.

Preheat the oven to 180°C (350°F/gas 4). Lightly butter a 900 g (2 lb) loaf tin and then sprinkle the breadcrumbs inside, shaking the tin to coat all the sides with the breadcrumbs.

Spoon the mixture into the prepared tin and bake in the oven for 1½ hours. Remove from the oven and let it completely cool and set. Serve thickly spread onto rye bread.

{Time: 4 hours and 30 minutes, plus soaking and cooling time}

In Poland, this is not called a Russian salad but an Italian salad, in remembrance of the Italian Queen Bona who ruled Poland in the 16th Century and brought with her Italian vegetables and cooking methods. Here, I give you my family's Russian salad, which we eat at every major celebration, with the addition of fresh crabmeat – a recent experiment that works beautifully and modernises this traditional recipe. **{Serves 6–8}**

A CELEBRATORY SLAVIC SALAD WITH CRABMEAT

2 parsnips
3 carrots
1 celeriac (celery root)
1 fresh leek
4 hard-boiled eggs, diced
1 x 175 g (6 oz) can peas, drained
4 gherkins, diced
400 ml (14 fl oz/1¾ cups) mayonnaise
1 teaspoon Dijon mustard
1 teaspoon caster (superfine) sugar
2 cooked crabs, shelled (ask the fishmonger to prepare these for you) or 2 x 170 g (6 oz) canned crabmeat
salt and white pepper, to taste
fresh chopped parsley, to serve

Bring a large pan of salted water to a boil and add the parsnips, carrots and celeriac. Cook for about 25 minutes, until tender but not mushy.

Drain and allow the vegetables to cool, then peel everything that needs peeling celeriac, carrots and parsnips. Chop all the large vegetables into tiny cubes – everything needs to be uniform in size, not much larger than a pea. Place in a bowl and add the diced hard-boiled eggs, peas, gherkins and leeks.

Mix the mayonnaise, mustard, sugar and salt and pepper together in a separate bowl. Add to the vegetables and mix together thoroughly.

Add the crabmeat at the end and mix it in gently.

Transfer the salad to a serving dish and smooth the surface with a spoon. Top with more mayonnaise to cover the vegetables entirely. Scatter with chopped parsley and serve with rye bread.

{Time: 1 hour, plus cooling time}

"The skill of making a genuinely Polish bigos is acquired through practice. It should be made with concentration and with frequent tasting in order to achieve the full harmony of artfully measured out ingredients. Haste and a distracted mind are particularly dangerous."

'Old Polish Traditions: In the Kitchen and at the Table' **{Serves 15}**

BIGOS (POLISH KIMCHI) WITH VENISON

100 g (3½ oz) dried wild mushrooms
5 tablespoons rapeseed oil
400 g (14 oz) pork belly, cubed
400 g (14 oz) stewing beef, cubed
1 onion, finely chopped
1.5 kg (3 lb 5 oz) sauerkraut (see page 251), drained
2 bay leaves
8–10 allspice berries
1 bottle of red wine
400 g (14 oz) venison, cubed
150 g (5 oz) Polish sausage, very small cubes
100 g (3½ oz) closed cup mushrooms, chopped
150 g (5 oz) prunes, pitted
1 tablespoon vegetable bouillon powder
1 tablespoon soy sauce
salt and black and white pepper, to taste

Day 1: Soak the dried mushrooms in a bowl of warm water for 30 minutes, then drain. Return to the bowl, pour boiling water over them and allow to stand for another 30 minutes.

Meanwhile, heat 2 tablespoons of the rapeseed oil in a very large pan and fry the pork belly for about 5 minutes, browning evenly. Add the beef and chopped onion and cook for a couple of minutes. Add the sauerkraut, bay leaves, allpsice berries, a glass of wine and enough water to cover the ingredients. Season with black and white pepper. Bring to a boil and then reduce the heat. Once the mushrooms have rehydrated, chop them into slithers, add them to the pan with their soaking liquid. Simmer for 2 hours.

The bigos will still be light in colour, but there should be no liquid in the pan. Allow it cool in the fridge overnight, or just allow to stand, covered, in a cool place.

Day 2: Pour 300 ml (10 fl oz/1¼ cups) of wine over the bigos and bring to a boil. When it begins to boil, reduce the heat to its lowest setting. Soak the venison cubes in a glass of the red wine and leave to marinate overnight. Meanwhile, fry the sausage for a few minutes in a tablespoon of oil, or until browned, and add to the bigos. Repeat with the mushrooms. Finally, add the prunes and cook for another 2 hours.

Day 3: Return the bigos to a medium heat and cook for about 2 hours with the remaining wine. When its evaporated add water every now and again, so its never dry. After 2 hours add the vegetable bouillon or soy sauce, then taste and adjust the seasoning with salt and pepper. Add the venison cubes, along with the wine they have been soaking in, to the bigos with 2 tablespoons of oil and cook for a further 30 minutes.

{Time: 9 hours, over 3 days}

CAKES AND DESSERTS

Dessert in Poland usually means cake. Patisseries thrive here because cake is such a major part of our culture and is eaten on a daily basis. This makes us all experts and it also means that general cake standards are kept high: only freshly baked cakes are considered acceptable. There also needs to be a clear balance of different flavours within our cakes, for example sweetness should be balanced out with tartness which in turn should be offset by creaminess. In Polish cuisine at least, an impressive cake means quite a bit of love and time has been put into making it. In this chapter there are a selection of cakes at both ends of the scale: quick and easy and more complicated ones, but they're all made with affection.

There is always an opportunity to eat cake in Poland. Whether you are popping into someone's house or even if your just picking something up, you will be offered tea or coffee and cake. If you are visiting a friend or relative, then it's polite to bring cake. If you're going out for a coffee then it's also very likely that you're going to eat a slice of cake. After a meal, you will always be served … you've guessed it – more cake.

It is fair to assume that many cakes originated from (or at the very least were influenced by) Poland's close contact with its ever-present foe. The popularity of almonds and almond extract in desserts certainly points to the Middle East.

There were many links between these two great forces over the centuries not least when Suleiman the Magnificent married a former slave girl from the Polish-Lithuanian Commonwealth, the influential Roxelana. However, the Ottoman Empire is not the only place where inspiration would have come from – as many cakes in Poland are reminiscent of those from Parisian patisseries, and it makes me wonder whether the great francophile King Jan III Sobiecki (who also won the Battle of Vienna and found all the leftover Turkish coffee) – imprinted his great love of France (and his lovely French wife) on our cuisine in the form of French confectionaries. What was popular in the king's court, after all, eventually trickled down to the populace.

The variety of cakes on offer is immense and we have cakes for every time of the year. During Easter we traditionally eat the lady-shaped *baba* cake and caramel *mazurek*, at Christmas it's time for poppy seeds and therefore *makowiec* rules, whereas in the summer we favour big meringue cakes with plenty of fresh fruit. We have cakes that hail from particular regions of the country and cannot be reproduced easily – the spectacular *sękacz* is made from such simple ingredients that it's a marvel that something so utterly delicious could be produced from its basic components. Of course, we also have many, many cakes that are popular the country over and beyond.

Black poppy seed cake looks strange and exotic if you're not used to it, yet if Poland had a national cake then this would be it. There's the traditional *makowiec* roll, the poppy-rich slice and even the *makowiec* cheesecake, yet this is a super-simple version which uses no dough at all. I wanted it to be fuss-free and this version has the added benefit of being quite healthy. Despite its simplicity it is still a rewarding process, as it takes time but only requires a small amount of effort. **{Serves 16}**

POPPY SEED AND ALMOND MAKOWIEC

400 g (14 oz) poppy seeds
200 g (7 oz/1 cup) brown sugar
50 ml (scant ¼ cup) brown rum
150 g (5 oz/1 cup) raisins
150 g (5 oz/1½ cups) flaked (slivered) almonds
2 teaspoons almond extract
4 egg yolks
2 tablespoons unsalted butter, softened
5 egg whites

FOR THE ICING

100 g (3½ oz/generous ¾ cup) icing (confectioners') sugar, sifted
1½ tablespoons lemon juice

Rinse the poppy seeds in water and add to a pan. Pour over enough boiling water to cover the seeds with ½ cm (¼ in) of water then place over a medium heat and simmer for 2–3 minutes. Turn off the heat, cover and leave to soak overnight.

The next day, preheat the oven to 190°C (375°F/gas 5) and line a 23 x 23 cm (9 x 9 in) round cake tin (pan) with baking paper (parchment paper).

Tip the poppy seeds into a food processor or blender and blitz until they start to produce poppy milk – you'll know when this happens because their colour will change slightly and they will appear lighter. It may take about half an hour. Meanwhile, soak the raisins in the rum in a small bowl for 20 minutes.

Combine the poppy seeds in a large bowl with all the other dry ingredients, then add the almond extract, egg yolks and butter and stir well.

In a separate bowl, beat the egg white until stiff peaks form. Gently fold the egg whites into the mixture and then pour it into the prepared cake tin. Bake in the oven for 40 minutes.

While it's baking, combine the icing sugar with the lemon juice to a thick drizzling consistency.

Allow the cake to cool in the tin. Drizzle the icing over the cake in any pattern you like.

{Time: 1 hour 10 minutes, plus overnight soaking time}

{Juicy Apple and Cinnamon *Szarlotka* with a Meringue Topping}

My grandma Halinka's cooking was not a great talent of hers and she always compared herself unfavourably to my grandma Ziuta, who had cooked for most of her life. Yet this recipe proves that even if your not a talented cook, you can still have your own speciality dishes: which become your own through practice, perseverance and love. After years of repetition and development they will become yours and you will live on through them as my grandma Halinka lives on through her *szarlotka*. **{Serves 12}**

JUICY APPLE AND CINNAMON SZARLOTKA WITH A MERINGUE TOPPING {see pages 210–211}

FOR THE DOUGH

- 500 g (1 lb 2 oz/4 cups) plain (all-purpose) flour
- 2 tablespoons soured cream
- 125 g (4 oz/½ cup) caster (superfine) sugar
- 125 g (4 oz/1 stick) unsalted butter
- 3 egg yolks
- 1 teaspoon baking powder

- 1 kg (1 lb 4 oz) cooking apples, peeled and coarsely grated
- 250 g (9 oz/1¼ cups) caster (superfine) sugar
- 1 tablespoon ground cinnamon
- 100 g (3½ oz/⅔ cup) raisins
- 4 egg whites
- 1 teaspoon vanilla extract

First make the dough. Combine the flour, soured cream, sugar, butter, egg yolks and baking powder together in a large bowl. Use your hands to bring the dough together. Once it comes away from your hand easily, take a handful of dough, and put it in a plastic bag and place in the freezer. Place the remaining dough in a separate plastic bag and chill in the fridge for at least 30 minutes.

Preheat the oven to 200°C (400°F/gas 6) and butter a 23 x 23 cm (9 x 9 in) round cake tin (pan).

Place the grated apple in a bowl with 25 g (2 tablespoons/ ⅛ cup) of the sugar, the cinnamon and raisins.

In a separate clean bowl, beat the egg whites to stiff peaks, then add the remaining sugar and vanilla extract and continue beating until the mixture thickens further.

Remove the dough from the fridge and roll it out in the plastic bag (it's a crumbly dough and this way it doesn't break so easily). Take it out of the bag and press into the cake tin, using your fingers to press it right to the edges. Ensure that the entire base of the tin is covered, if it breaks at all just press it back together. Bake in the oven for 10 minutes then remove from the oven and spread the apple mixture evenly on top of the dough. Return to the oven for a further 10 minutes.

Remove the cake from the oven and lower the oven temperature to 160°C (325°F/gas 3). Top the apples with the egg white mixture, then take the smaller ball of dough from the freezer and grate that over the top. Return the cake to the oven and bake for 30 minutes, or until the topping is golden.

Allow to cool slightly before serving.

{Time: 50 minutes, plus resting time}

Karpatka and *Napoleonka* are very similar cream cakes, however they use two different types of pastry. The pastry used for a *Karpatka* is mountainous, as befitting a cake named after the Karpaty mountain range. *Napoleonka* on the other hand uses French pastry and is named after Plac Napoleona – Napoleon's Square in Warsaw where it was first sold. This cake is more of a *Karpatka* because the pastry becomes hilly if not mountainous. The cardamom adds an exotic, old-world twist. If you don't have much time but would still like to give this cake a go, then you can simply turn it into a *Napoleonka* cake by using ready-made puff pastry. **{Serves 20}**

CARDAMOM AND VANILLA KARPATKA CREAM CAKE

FOR THE DOUGH

150 ml (5 fl oz/⅔ cup) water
80 g (3 oz/6 tablespoons) salted butter
180 g (6½ oz/scant 1½ cups) plain (all-purpose) flour
¼ teaspoon bicarbonate of soda (baking soda)
4 eggs

FOR THE FILLING

500 ml (18 fl oz/2 cups) milk
50 ml (2 fl oz/scant ¼ cup) single (light) cream
5 cardamom pods
1 vanilla pod (bean), slit lengthways
100 g (3½ oz/½ cup) soft light brown sugar
4 egg yolks
4 tablespoons cornflour (cornstarch)
200 g (7 oz/scant 1 cup) softened unsalted butter
icing (confectioners') sugar, for dusting

Make the dough by placing the water in a pan with the butter. Melt over a low heat; once it's melted, start sifting in the flour and bicarbonate of soda while stirring all the time. Make sure the flour is thoroughly blended with no lumps, then allow it to cool.

Preheat the oven to 200°C (400°F/gas 6) and line a large baking tray with baking paper (parchment paper).

Once the dough is at room temperature, add the eggs and mix in thoroughly. Blend it for a few minutes – it will remain sticky but don't worry. Spread the dough as thinly as you can on to the prepared baking tray and bake in the oven for 30 minutes. Remove from the oven and allow to cool on a wire rack.

Now make the filling. Place 400 ml (14 fl oz/1¾ cups) of the milk in a pan with the cream, cardamom pods and vanilla pod. Place over a low heat and heat until just scalding. Just before it comes to a boil remove from the heat and set aside to infuse with the flavours of the cardamom and vanilla.

Meanwhile, whisk the sugar and egg yolks together to create a smooth paste. Blend the cornflour with the remaining milk and add to the egg and sugar mixture and carry on whisking. Strain the infused milk and cream into the egg mixture, whisking as you go (discard the cardamom and vanilla pods). Pour this mixture back into the pan and place over a low heat. Stir continuously until it thickens, for about 10 minutes. Once the mixture is very thick – it should be an effort to stir now – take it off the heat and place the pan in a sink of cold water to cool, stirring occasionally. Once the mixture is completely cold and stiff, blend it with a hand-held electric whisk while adding the butter, a little at a time.

Cut the cooled pastry in half. Spread the filling over one half of the pastry and then top with the other half. Dust with icing sugar before serving.

{Time: 1 hour 10 minutes, plus cooling time}

This cheesecake is based on my grandma Ziuta's recipe. Make sure you use organic oranges and lemons as you need a lot of zest to get the necessary citrusy flavour and you want it to be as pure and nutritious as possible. The more egg whites you put in the fluffier the consistency. I've been known to put in 10 egg whites to 6 yolks and, personally, I love that extra-fluffy texture. I haven't gone crazy with the amounts of egg whites in this recipe, but if you like fluffiness and have extra whites then they certainly won't hurt! **{Serves 20}**

TANGY TWO-CITRUS CHEESECAKE

FOR THE DOUGH

125 g (4 oz/1 stick) unsalted butter
2 egg yolks
500 g (1 lb 2 oz/4 cups) plain (all-purpose) flour
1 teaspoon baking powder
2 tablespoons soured cream
125 g (4½ oz/generous ½ cup) caster (superfine) sugar

FOR THE FILLING

6–8 egg yolks
200 g (7 oz/1½ cups) sugar
1 kg (2 lb 3 oz) soft white cheese
200 g (7 oz/scant 1 cup) unsalted butter, softened
2 tablespoons finely grated orange zest
2 tablespoons finely grated lemon zest
1 teaspoon vanilla extract
6–8 egg whites

FOR THE ICING

200 g (7 oz/1¾ cups) icing (confectioners') sugar
juice of ½ lemon
juice of ½ orange

Combine all the ingredients for the dough in a large bowl and knead them together into a smooth ball for 10 minutes. When the ball no longer sticks to your hands, it's ready. Pop it into a large plastic food bag and chill in the fridge for about 20 minutes.

Preheat the oven to 180°C (350°F/gas 4) and lightly grease a 24 cm (9½ in) sqaure cake tin (pan).

To make the filling, blend the egg yolks and sugar in bowl until you have a light coloured, smooth paste. Slowly add the cheese and butter by adding a tablespoon of one, then a tablespoon of the other, beating well between each addition. Beat in the orange and lemon zest and vanilla extract. In another bowl, beat the egg whites to stiff peaks. Gently fold into filling mixture.

Take the dough out of the fridge and cut off about two-thirds. Roll the larger piece out and cut it into a square which fits the entire base of your baking tray. Bake in the oven for 10 minutes.

Meanwhile, roll out the smaller piece as thinly as you can and cut it into strips about 1 cm (½ in) wide.

Remove the cooked base from the oven then lower the oven temperature to 160°C (325°F/gas 3). Allow to cool slightly before pouring over the cheesecake mixture. Lay the dough strips over the top, making stripes or checks as you prefer. Bake in the oven for about 50–60 minutes, or until evenly golden all over.

While the cheesecake is baking, make the icing. Sift the icing sugar into a bowl and add the lemon and orange juices. It needs to be quite thick so don't add all the juice at once; pour the juice in slowly and mix it together until it reaches a runny consistency while sticking to a spoon. Brush the icing between the checks or stripes while the cake is still warm. Leave to cool completely before serving.

(Time: 1 hour 30 minutes, plus cooling and chilling time)

Carnival time, among the rich and poor alike, is a partying endurance test. This tradition continues the week before Lent as it is filled with food, drink and dancing. These *faworki* cakes are made from all the ingredients you want to use before the Lenten fasting begins. **{Makes 20 *faworki*}**

FAWORKI CARNIVAL CAKES WITH A TWIST

- 250 g (9 oz/2 cups) plain (all-purpose) flour
- 3 tablespoons crème fraîche
- 3 egg yolks
- 50 g (1¾ oz/3½ tablespoons) salted butter
- 1 tablespoon icing (confectioners') sugar, plus extra to serve
- 2 tablespoons lemon vodka, or other strong spirit or lemon juice
- 500 ml (18 fl oz/2 cups) rapeseed oil, for frying

Sift the flour into a bowl and add the crème fraîche, egg yolks, butter and icing sugar. I have used lemon vodka as the liquid element but you could use any other spirit or lemon juice. Mix together and then knead the dough for about 4–5 minutes, until smooth.

Roll the dough out as thinly as you can on a lightly floured surface. Cut the dough into rectangular shapes, about 9 x 4 cm (3½ x 1½ in). Cut a slit about 3 cm (1¼ in) long in the middle of each one. Now weave one end through the slit and pull it through to achieve the desired shape.

Pour the oil for frying into a large, heavy-based pan. Heat to 180°C (350°F); if you don't have a kitchen thermometer you can test the temperature by dropping in a small piece of dough: if it sizzles immediately, then your oil is ready. Deep-fry these for about 30 seconds each side, or until golden. Remove from the pan with a slotted spoon, drain on kitchen paper (paper towels) and dust with icing sugar while still warm. Serve immediately.

{Time: 30 minutes}

Although making *mazurek* does take time it is a very simple recipe. If you would like to simplify the pastry then you can use ready-made caramel or dulce de leche, though the consistency will be a little bit more runny. In my recipe, I have replaced the traditional hazelnuts and walnuts with salted pecans and I have also added some sea salt to the caramel to balance out its all-consuming sweetness. **{Makes 10 portions}**

SALTED CARAMEL MAZUREK WITH PECANS

FOR THE DOUGH:

300 g (10½ oz/scant 2½ cups) plain (all-purpose) flour
125 g (4½ oz/⅔ cup) soft light brown sugar
200 g (7 oz/scant 1 cup) salted butter, softened
2 egg yolks
½ teaspoon vanilla extract
1 tablespoon soured cream

FOR THE FILLING:

1 x 400 g (400 fl oz) can condensed milk
25 g (scant 1 oz/2 tablespoons) salted butter
25 g (scant 1 oz/2 tablespoons) soft light brown sugar
100 g (3½ oz/⅔ cup) pecans, broken up into smaller pieces
½ teaspoon good-quality sea salt

For the filling place a can of condensed milk in a pan of water, making sure it is completely covered. Bring the water to a boil then reduce the heat right down to the lowest setting and simmer for 3 hours. Top up with extra water if it evaporates.

Meanwhile, combine the flour, sugar and butter in a bowl and work between your fingertips until it resembles breadcrumbs. Add the egg yolks, vanilla extract and soured cream and knead together into a smooth dough. Chill in the fridge for 30–45 minutes.

Preheat the oven to 180°C (350°F/gas 4). Roll out the dough on a lightly floured surface to a thickness of about 1 cm (½ in). Use this to line a greased brownie tin, approximately 24 cm (9½ in). Bake in the oven for 15–20 minutes, or until golden. Remove and allow to cool.

Meanwhile, in a frying pan (skillet) melt the butter and sugar together over a low heat, then add the pecans and most of the sea salt. Toast for a few minutes, stirring all the time. Set aside.

Once the condensed milk has turned to caramel and cooled to nearly room temperature, open the can and stir a little bit more salt into it, reserving a little bit for the topping.

Spread the caramel over the cooled base generously and top with the caramelised pecans. Sprinkle over a little more sea salt before serving.

{Time: 3 hours 30 minutes, plus chilling time}

Polish doughnuts have been loved for centuries and in this recipe I have used a traditional rose petal jam filling. You can source it online or make it yourself in June when the wild roses are in bloom (see page 252). If you would like to replace the rose petal jam with another kind, may I suggest something not too sweet; plum jam would be a good choice.

Rectified spirit is 95 per cent alcohol and often used for the task of cake making, however, if this is not something you have to hand use a clear vodka or rum instead. There is nothing quite like the taste of a still-warm, bouncy *pączek* with a delicately fragrant filling melting in your mouth. **{Makes 16–20}**

AROMATIC DOUGHNUTS WITH AN OLD-STYLE ROSE FILLING

FOR THE DOUGH

250 ml (8 fl oz/1 cup) milk
25 g (scant 1 oz) fresh yeast
75 g (2 oz) caster (superfine) sugar
500 g (1 lb 2 oz/4 cups) good-quality plain (all-purpose) flour
3 egg yolks
½ vanilla pod (bean)
1 tablespoon softened unsalted butter
25 ml (1 fl oz/2 tablespoons) vodka

2 litres (3½ pints/8 cups) rapeseed oil, for frying

FOR THE FILLING

400 g (14 oz) rose petal jam (see page 252), (1 teaspoon of jam per doughnut)

TO GLAZE

100 g (3½ oz/generous ¾ cup) icing (confectioners') sugar
3 tablespoons lemon juice

Gently heat 50 ml (2 fl oz/¼ cup) of the milk in a small pan. Once it is warm (but not hot), place in a bowl with the fresh yeast, a tablespoon of the sugar and 3 tablespoons of flour and mix well together. Cover with a tea towel (dish towel) and leave to rest in a warm place for 30 minutes (ideally near a radiator).

Sift the remaining flour into a large bowl and add the rest of the dough ingredients. Work it together with the milk and yeast mixture until the rough shape of a ball is formed. Knead it for a few minutes, to get some air into it, then cover the bowl with a tea towel and return to your warm place, for at least 1 hour, or until it has doubled in size.

Get everything ready to make your doughnuts: dust a large tray or plate with flour and have a cup of warm water and a spoon at the ready, plus a plate of flour to dip the balls of dough (and your hands) into. Knead the dough ball for a moment longer to see how sticky it is; although it should be sticky you do need to be able to work with it so keep your hands dusted with flour as you work. Take a small piece of dough, roll it into a ball and flatten it out with your other (floured) hand to a circle that is about 8–10 cm (3–4 in) in diameter. Try not to add too much additional flour to the dough, otherwise the dough will become too heavy.

Place ½ teaspoonful of rose petal jam into the middle of each flat circle. Seal the circle and roll it between your hands to make a ball. Place on the flour-dusted tray and repeat this process until you have used up all the dough. Cover them with a tea towel and return to a warm place for about 30–40 minutes, or until they have doubled in size.

Meanwhile, make the glaze by combining the icing sugar and lemon juice, blend the mixture until it reaches an completely smooth consistency.

When the doughnuts have doubled in size pour the oil for frying into a large, heavy-based pan. Heat to 180°C (350°F);

if you don't have a kitchen thermometer you can test the temperature after about 20 minutes by dropping in a small piece of dough: if it sizzles immediately, and becomes golden within 45 seconds, then your oil is ready.

Place each doughnut carefully into the oil using a slotted spoon, making sure you do not splash yourself with the oil and no droplets of water goes near it. Fry the doughnuts, in batches, until they are a golden brown colour on both sides. This takes about 5 minutes on each side at first, but as the oil becomes hotter they will take less time to cook.

Remove them carefully with a slotted spoon and transfer to a plate or tray lined with kitchen paper (paper towel). Use a pastry brush to glaze the doughnuts while they are still warm, so that the icing melts evenly all over them and makes them shiny.

Serve as soon as possible. Although they are perfectly delicious the next day, you should at least have one or two while they are still warm.

{Time: 1 hour, plus resting time}

Anyone could order a torte from my grandma Ziuta, and everyone did. She often made more than one a week and asked for no payment, creating each one with care, decorating them with pastel coloured icing, marzipan flowers and most importantly, love. They were the most colourful, wondrous thing to behold in grey Communist Poland.

Ideally, loose tea leaves should be used, but if you don't have them than a good-quality tea bag is fine – and be generous with it! **{Serves 12–16}**

BOOZY CHOCOLATE AND WALNUT TORTE

Preheat the oven to 180°C (350°F/gas 4) and grease a loose-bottomed 23 x 23 cm (9 x 9 in) round cake tin (pan). Sprinkle the inside of the tin with the breadcrumbs.

Place the egg whites in a clean bowl and whisk until stiff peaks form. Gradually add the icing sugar and whisk until they have combined and become considerably thicker. Add the egg yolks and whisk again. Gently fold in the flour (mixed with the baking powder), add the cocoa powder and vanilla extract or inside of a vanilla pod, mixing gently, then pour into your prepared tin. Bake in the oven for 50 minutes, or until a skewer comes out clean. If it is not baked through, return the cake to the oven, turn the oven off and leave inside for 7–8 minutes. Leave it to cool in the tin for a few minutes and then turn out onto a wire rack to cool completely.

Meanwhile, make the icing by blending the egg yolks and sugar together, then adding the butter, a little at a time, and finally the chocolate paste and vanilla. Place this thick mass in the fridge for about 20 minutes to chill.

To make the walnut cream filling, whip the cream to soft peaks, then gradually add the sugar and keep whisking until you have stiff peaks. Fold in the finely ground walnuts. Using a bread knife, carefully slice the cake horizontally into three equal layers (don't attempt this while the cake is still warm as it will be too crumbly). Add the rum to the cooled, sweet tea and then use this syrup to thoroughly soak the first sponge layer. Spread about half of the walnut cream filling over the top and then repeat with the next layer of sponge, soaking with syrup and spreading with the remaining walnut cream.

Smear the chocolate icing over the top of the final layer and down the sides to cover the entire cake, as thick as you like. Decorate the sides of the cake with walnuts and almonds.

{Time: 1 hour 50 minutes, plus chilling}

FOR THE CAKE

1 tablespoon dried breadcrumbs
8 eggs, separated
250 g (9 oz/2 cups) icing (confectioners') sugar
250 g (9 oz/2 cups) plain (all-purpose) flour
1 teaspoon baking powder
1 tablespoon cocoa powder
½ vanilla pod (bean) or 1 teaspoon vanilla extract

FOR THE CHOCOLATE ICING

2 egg yolks
100 g (3½ oz/generous ¾ cup) icing (confectioners') sugar
200 g (7 oz/scant 1 cup) unsalted butter, softened
50 g (1¾ oz/½ cup) good-quality cocoa powder blended to a paste with 5 tablespoons boiled water
seeds from ½ vanilla pod (bean) or 1 teaspoon vanilla extract

FOR THE WALNUT CREAM

100 ml (3½ fl oz/scant ½ cup) whipping cream
200 g (7 oz/1⅔ cup cups) icing (confectioners') sugar
200 g (7 oz/2½ cups) walnuts, ground

FOR THE SYRUP

75 ml (2½ fl oz/⅓ cup) very strong tea with 2 tablespoons brown sugar
75 ml (2½ fl oz/⅓ cup) dark rum

TO DECORATE

100 g (3½ oz/1 cup) walnuts, some crushed and some left whole
100 g (3½ oz/1 cup) flaked (slivered) almonds

PRZEMYSŁU

Biting into a caramel pine cone always makes me think of biting into a bees' nest. I have added sesame seeds to the recipe which makes this recipe a cross between my two favourite Polish sweet snacks: *szyszki* and *sezamki*. These light-as-air rice cakes are made with the popular Polish sweet: *krówki* (little cows), which you can buy in all Polish shops and in the Polish section of supermarkets too. In a Polish shop this rice would be called *ryż preparowany*. I've found a brown rice cereal in the gluten-free section of my local supermarket which is a good substitute as are other cereals as long as they are quite solid and strong, as they need to withstand both the hot fudge and the moulding process. **{Makes 20}**

CRUNCHY PINE CONES

100 g (3½ oz) sesame seeds
100 g (3½ oz/7 tablespoons) unsalted butter
200 g (7 oz) *krówki* sweets (or equivalent cream fudge sweets)
100 g (3½ oz) strong puffed rice or other cereal

Lightly toast the sesame seeds in a dry frying pan (skillet) and set aside.

Melt the butter in a pan and start to add the *krówki*, mixing them together as they get softer. Eventually they will melt into one caramel coloured mass. Remove from the heat and add the toasted sesame seeds, followed by the puffed rice.

Mix together well with a wooden spoon, then wait a little while (approximately 10 minutes, but check yourself when you're happy to work with the mass without burning your hands, remembering that the inside is always warmer) before forming into pine cone shapes. Have some cold water on standby to dip your hands into.

Allow to cool and harden completely before serving.

{Time: 30 minutes}

The Polish and Ashkenazi Jewish cuisines developed alongside each other in this part of the world for over 800 years, therefore at times it is difficult to pinpoint what came from where, yet this pretty dessert is known to be of Jewish origin. You will need a large piece of gauze or muslin to make this dessert. **{Makes 20}**

JEWISH-STYLE PASCHA DESSERT

250 g (9 oz/1 cup) unsalted butter
200 g (7 oz/scant 1 cup) caster (superfine) sugar
4 egg yolks
1.5 kg (3 lb 5 oz) *twaróg* or ricotta
300 ml (10 fl oz/1¼ cups) single (light) cream
1 vanilla pod (bean), slit lengthways
150 g (5 oz/1½ cups) flaked (slivered) almonds
50 g (1¾ oz/¼ cup) sultanas (golden raisins)
50 g (1¾ oz) pitted dates, chopped
50 g (1¾ oz) candied orange peel
cornflowers, to decorate (optional)

Cream together the butter and sugar, either in a bowl with a wooden spoon or using an electric mixer. Slowly add the egg yolks and the white cheese by adding a little bit of one followed by a little bit of the other, beating well between each addition.

Finally, add the cream and vanilla pod and pour the mixture into a pan. Bring this mixture very slowly up to a boil, stirring continuously (this may take up to 25 minutes). Meanwhile, toast the flaked almonds in a dry frying pan (skillet).

Once bubbles start to appear in the cream mixture, add the dried fruit, candied peel and toasted almonds.

Now comes the slightly complicated part of the process: you need to line a 23 x 23 cm (9 x 9 in) cake mould with the muslin (cheesecloth) or gauze material, leaving enough around the sides to cover the top. Pour the mixture into the lined mould and fold the muslin over the top. Once the mixture has cooled slightly, place a plate on top, flip your mould over and weigh it down with something heavy – a can is ideal.

Place it in the fridge to chill and set for at least 8 hours, preferably 12–24 hours.

Decorate by scattering edible cornflowers whimsically over the top.

{Time: 45 minutes, plus setting time}

Kisiel is one of those tangy, refreshing desserts, which makes you wince at its tartness and yet keeps you going back for more. The meringue clouds and cream bring a necessary sweet relief to the sour fruit.

Kisiel is something my generation grew up on because although it's a sweet dessert, it contains a lot of fruit-based vitamins and it's very straightforward to make. The main ingredient is fresh, seasonal fruit, such as gooseberries, wild cherries or raspberries. I've given two *kisiel* variations here using different ingredients – the method is the same so just choose which flavour you prefer. **{Serves 6–8}**

WHIMSICAL, FRUITY KISIEL WITH MERINGUE CLOUDS {see pages 228–229}

FOR THE MERINGUES

2 egg whites
pinch of salt
100 g (3½ oz/½ cup) caster (superfine) sugar
½ teaspoon vanilla extract

VARIATION 1: RASPBERRY

2 heaped tablespoons potato flour or cornflour (cornstarch)
400 ml (14 fl oz/1¾ cups) filtered water
400 g (14 oz/3¼ cups) fresh raspberries, plus extra to decorate
100 g (3½ oz/scant ½ cup) caster (superfine) sugar
juice of ½ lemon

VARIATION 2 : GOOSEBERRY

2 heaped tablespoons potato flour or cornflour (cornstarch)
400 ml (14 fl oz/1¾ cups) filtered water
400 g (14 oz) fresh gooseberries
100 g (3½ oz/scant ½ cup) caster (superfine) sugar
1 teaspoon vanilla extract
redcurrants, to decorate

100 ml (3½ fl oz/scant ½ cup) whipping cream

First make the meringues. Preheat the oven to 120°C (240°C/gas ½) and line a baking tray with baking paper (parchment paper).

Whisk the egg whites and salt together in a very clean bowl until stiff peaks form. Gradually add the sugar and vanilla extract, whisking all the time until you have a thick, glossy mixture. Spoon the mixture into a piping (pastry) bag fitted with a plain round nozzle (tip) and pipe at least 12 small 'clouds' on to the lined baking tray. Bake in the oven for 1½ hours, until crisp. Leave them to cool in the oven with the door ajar.

Combine the potato flour or cornflour with half of the water and mix well until smooth. Put the remaining water in a pan and bring to a boil. When the water is boiling, add the water with the flour in it, and keep stirring while it thickens.

Put the fruit and sugar into a food processor or blender with the lemon juice or vanilla, depending on which variation you are using. Blitz briefly – you are not looking for a smooth purée and some fruity bits should remain.

Once the floured water has simmered for 2 minutes and thickened considerably add the fruity mixture. Bring this to a boil and cook, stirring, for 1 minute, then remove from the heat.

Rinse your serving bowls with cold water and pour this mixture into them, in order to help the *kisiel* set. Allow to cool, then chill in the fridge for at least 30 minutes.

To serve, whip the cream to stiff peaks and place 2–3 dollops in each bowl, on top of the *kisiel*. Top with a meringue cloud or two and decorate with fresh fruit.

{Time: 2 hours, plus cooling and chilling time}

Pobożnik is a very rare cake indeed. Not many people have even heard of it, however my mum's cousin, Ania Majewska, mentioned that I should put it in this book and she sent me this recipe that had been jotted down from her mother's (grandma Zosia, my grandma Ziuta's little sister) slightly dusty memory of it. It's like a tiramisu but more cakey in appearance. **{Serves 12}**

POBOŻNIK HOLY SEMOLINA LAYERED CAKE

Preheat the oven to 180°C (350°F/gas 4). Grease three identical round tins, about 23 x 23 cm (9 x 9 in) in diameter.

Combine all the ingredients for the dough in a large bowl and knead them together, then divide into three portions. Roll each one to 1 cm (½ in) height and place in the prepared tins. Bake for 40 minutes, until a deep golden colour. Leave to cool in the tins for about 10 minutes, then carefully remove from the tins and allow to cool completely.

Meanwhile make the filling. Blend the semolina in a bowl with a little bit of cold water and mix to a smooth paste. Meanwhile put the milk into a pan and heat gently until just scalding. Pour the semolina paste slowly into the hot milk and simmer together for a couple of minutes. Remove from the heat and allow to cool and thicken – you could speed up the process by putting the pan in a bath of cold water.

Once it's completely cooled, blend it with the sugar, butter, lemon juice, vanilla extract and salt, adding all the ingredients in gradually, while you blend.

Make the chocolate topping by placing the cocoa powder, sugar, butter and water in a pan and heat gently. Stir and simmer until smooth and thick, then allow to cool.

Cut each cake in half with a sharp knife, so that you now have six layers. Place on a plate and then assemble the cake by spreading plenty of semolina cream between each later. Finish off with the chocolate sauce and pecans: pour the sauce over the top of the cake and allow it to dribble down the sides, then sprinkle pecan pieces all over the top of the cake.

{Time: 1 hour, plus resting time}

FOR THE DOUGH

600 g (1 lb 5 oz/generous 4¾ cups) plain (all-purpose) flour
300 g (10½ oz/1½ cups) caster (superfine) sugar
2 eggs
125 g (4½ oz/1 stick) unsalted butter
2 tablespoons honey
2–3 tablespoons milk
1 teaspoon bicarbonate of soda (baking soda)

FOR THE FILLING

8 tablespoons semolina
500 ml (18 fl oz/2 cups) milk
200 g (7 oz/1 cup) caster (superfine) sugar
200 g (7 oz/scant 1 cup) unsalted butter
juice of 1 lemon
1 teaspoon vanilla extract
pinch of salt

FOR THE CHOCOLATE SAUCE

50 g (1¾ oz/½ cup) cocoa powder
150 g (5 oz/¾ cup) caster (superfine) sugar
120 g (4 oz/½ cup) unsalted butter
2–3 tablespoons water

handful pecan pieces, toasted

COCKTAILS

Drinking neat vodka while eating *zakąski* is a Polish tradition, however, our wide variety of vodkas lend themselves readily to the creation of many fantastic cocktails.

A few years ago, *Żubrówka* was a rarity, now it's on sale in many supermarkets, as is the high quality, clear *Belvedere* vodka. *Krupnik* (honey vodka) and *Żołądkówka Gorzka* (a bitter, digestif vodka, which is actually quite sweet) are less common, yet still available online. These are a good starting point, but there are many, many more wonderful vodkas from Eastern Europe, waiting to be discovered by the rest of the world. One of my favourites is the Ukrainian honey and chilli vodka, which cuts through warm food wonderfully. I was introduced to this when I was a student making the most of my long holidays in Poland. We were on the Ukrainian border visiting an artist friend who lived in an artfully dilapidated manor house, and we drank this honey and chilli vodka while eating a simple potato and cheese pie while we watched the sun set over glistening wheat fields on the horizon.

Some of these cocktail recipes are taken from my father's cocktail repertoire, others are modernised interpretations of Polish cocktail classics and there are a few of my own invention thrown in for good measure. Unless otherwise stated the measurements are for one cocktail but you'll probably want to double or triple them to make more than one cocktail at a time. You will need a cocktail shaker for many of them, but you can also use a large clean jar and a small sieve. If you choose to adopt the makeshift cocktail shaker, put some ice cubes in a lidded jar along with all the ingredients, close the lid and shake. Use a small sieve to strain the cocktail into a glass.

My dad habitually heats his *Krupnik* in the microwave, but I once managed to convince him to do it on the stove. The vodka somehow caught on fire in the pan and when my father attempted to blow the fire out, it instead blew into his face and enveloped his whole head. He singed his eyebrows and his face was very red, but luckily no permanent damage was done. Lesson learnt, if you would like to heat *Krupnik* please use a microwave – about 20 seconds should suffice. Otherwise, just make this cocktail, which is a far less hazardous way of drinking this old-fashioned vodka. **{Serves 1}**

SLAVIC REMEDY

Combine all the ingredients in a tall glass and mix well with a spoon. Serve with ice and a slice of lemon.

- 50 ml (2 fl oz/¼ cup) *Krupnik* honey vodka
- 200 ml (7 fl oz/scant 1 cup) ginger ale
- splash of Angostura bitters
- squeeze of lemon juice
- slice of lemon

If we had a national cocktail, then this would be it! *Żubrówka* and apple juice is by far the most popular combination in Poland for a very good reason. Even without the cinnamon it tastes divine; add the cinnamon and you magically have apple pie in a glass. I say magically because *Zubrówka* by itself has a rather bitter, herbal taste, yet the apple juice transforms it. In turn, the vodka adds depth and balances out the sweetness of the apple. **{Serves 1}**

APPLE PIE

Combine the ingredients in a tall glass and serve over ice.

- 50 ml (2 fl oz/¼ cup) *Żubrówka* Bison Grass vodka
- 200 ml (7 fl oz/scant 1 cup) good-quality apple juice
- large pinch of ground cinnamon

People in Poland often make their own vodkas using rectified spirit for medicinal purposes. My grandma Ziuta always had *Orzechówka* (a bitter-tasting nut vodka) on hand, which she used to treat stomach complaints with. You can easily infuse ordinary vodka with spices and I've found that this cardamom infusion is particularly lovely. Add some cardamom pods to a bottle of vodka, seal it and leave it at room temperature (turning the bottle once a day). Within four or five days the cardamom flavour will have developed, but I like to leave it even longer – a week or two – before using it in this cocktail. **{Serves 1}**

SPICED CHOCOLATE MARTINI

50 g (1¾ oz) good-quality dark chocolate
50 ml (2 fl oz/scant ¼ cup) single (light) cream
large pinch of ground cinnamon, plus extra to serve
100 ml (3½ fl oz/scant ½ cup) cardamom-infused vodka (see method above)

Place the chocolate in a heatproof bowl and set over a pan of gently simmering water, making sure the bottom of the bowl doesn't touch the water. As soon as it has melted remove from the heat and whisk in the cream and cinnamon.

Allow to cool completely before shaking it in a cocktail shaker with the vodka over ice, then pour it into a martini glass. Alternatively, shake in a jam jar and strain into a glass.

Sprinkle over a little more ground cinnamon before serving.

Avocado S.A.
Advocaat was the first alcoholic drink I ever tried. My grandma Halinka used to give me some in the bottom of a shot glass whenever she had guests round. They would sit around her polished oak table, drinking tea, eating cake and sipping on this sunny-coloured liquor, discussing grown-up matters. I would dip my finger in the advocaat and lick it off thoughtfully while pretending to understand their conversations. **{Serves 1}**

THE SNOWFLAKE

125 ml (4 fl oz/½ cup) sparkling wine, such as Prosecco or Cava

FOR THE HOMEMADE ADVOCAAT

300 ml (10 fl oz/1¼ cups) milk
1 vanilla pod (bean), slit lengthways
5–6 egg yolks
200 g (7 oz/1 cup) caster (superfine) sugar
300 ml (10 fl oz/1¼ cups) good-quality vodka

First make your homemade advocaat. Place the milk in a pan with the vanilla pod and heat gently until it just comes to a boil. Leave to infuse and cool completely.

While it's cooling whisk the egg yolks with the sugar until smooth and creamy. Pour the egg yolk mixture into the cool milk, whisking all the time, to make a sort of custard.

Add the vodka, whisk for another 2 minutes, then pour the mixture into a clean bottle or jar and leave for 5 days. Store in the fridge for up to 1 month.

To make the cocktail, pour a little of your homemade advocaat into a champagne glass and top up with sparkling wine.

A sour is basically the cocktail equivalent of a lemon meringue pie. A proper sour needs half a raw egg white in it, as it gives the drink its signature fluffy consistency. It's important to shake the egg white really well – for as long as you possibly can (do take breaks if you need to). It is worth doubling the quantities, so you make two cocktails at a time with one egg white. **{Serves 1}**

KRUPNIK SOUR

Combine the ingredients in a cocktail shaker and shake for at least 5 minutes, longer if you can manage it. Serve in a short glass over ice.

50 ml (2 fl oz/scant ¼ cup) *Krupnik* vodka (MADE OF POTATOS)
juice of 1 lemon
½ egg white
1 tablespoon runny honey or golden (corn) syrup → SOUTH AMERICAN
½ teaspoon vanilla extract → MEXICAN

[Bloody Bison] [Rosemary and Thyme Aperitif]

A Tudor King Henry VIII and Queen Catalina (Catherine) of Aragon daughter, Queen Mery (Maria) caused discontent as a Catholic in a Church of England country, G.B., so she became to known as bloody Mery.

No one knows exactly where the Bloody Mary originated from. However, there is a legend that it was created by a Polish barman working in a New York nightclub in the 1930s. I choose to believe this story because the cocktail combines vodka and horseradish, which has Polish taste written all over it! **{Serves 1}**

BLOODY BISON {see page 242}

50 ml (2 fl oz/scant ¼ cup) *Żubrówka* Bison Grass vodka
½ teaspoon horseradish sauce
splash of Worcestershire sauce
pinch of salt
pinch of white pepper
200 ml (7 fl oz/scant 1 cup) tomato juice
splash of Tabasco sauce (or to taste)
celery stalk
carrot stick

In a tall glass, mix the vodka, horseradish, Worcestershire sauce, salt and pepper then top up with tomato juice. Add some ice and as much Tabasco as you fancy. Finish with a stalk of celery and a stick of carrot.

Żołądkówka is one of my favourite vodkas. It's called bitter vodka – *gorzka* – yet confusingly it's actually quite sweet and very easy to drink on its own. If you like to drink neat vodka shots, then your vodka should always be kept in the freezer and served very cold and gloopy. Otherwise, this particular vodka is delicious with tonic – again offsetting sweetness with bitterness. **{Serves 1}**

ROSEMARY AND THYME APERITIF {see page 243}

½ tablespoon fresh thyme
½ tablespoon fresh rosemary
splash of lemon juice
splash of Angostura bitters
50 ml (2 fl oz/scant ¼ cup) *Żołądkówka* vodka
200 ml (7 fl oz/scant 1 cup) Indian tonic water
rosemary and thyme sprigs, to decorate

Using a pint glass and a pestle (or rolling pin) grind (mull) the thyme, rosemary, lemon juice, Angostura bitters and vodka together. This should take 3–4 minutes.

Strain through a sieve into a glass filled with ice and top up with tonic water. Decorate each glass with a sprig of rosemary and thyme.

Bilberries are a woodland fruit that are so full of flavour and colour that they dye your mouth black when you eat them. Blueberries are less potent in comparison, but if you cannot get hold of bilberries then do use blackberries instead. **{Serves 1}**

BILBERRY CAPRIOSKA

2 tablespoons bilberries or blackberries
1 tablespoon brown sugar
50 ml (2 fl oz/scant ¼ cup) good-quality vodka
½ lime, quartered
50–100 ml (2–3½ fl oz/scant ¼–½ cup) soda water

Add the bilberries, brown sugar and vodka into a blender and roughly blitz. Then with a pestle and mortar, grind (mull) the lime quarters. Mix the lime juice and lime pieces into the blended mixture. Fill a tall glass with crushed ice and pour the cocktail over the top. Top up with soda water, mix gently and serve.

Mulled beer is a popular drink during cold winter days – especially in the mountains. There are various ways of making it, but my dad's version (which has a whisked egg in it) is the best. This recipe is actually similar to a medieval beer soup that Poles used to consume for breakfast.

Although this is my favourite recipe, there are far simpler ones. For instance, in the Polish mountains, they drink dark beer, heated with cinnamon, nutmeg and honey – which is also very good. **{Serves 4}**

TATRAS WINTER WARMER – CREAMY MULLED BEER

4 light beer cans
1 tablespoon ground cinnamon
1 teaspoon cloves
3 eggs, separated
pinch of salt
2 tablespoons light brown sugar
2 tablespoons honey
1 tablespoon vanilla extract
1 tablespoon brandy

Put the beer, cinnamon and cloves into a pan and place over a very gentle heat, stirring all the time. Once it is warm (but not hot), cover it, remove from the heat and allow it to infuse with the spices for 10 minutes.

Whisk the egg whites with a pinch of salt until stiff peaks form. Blend the yolks with the sugar in a separate bowl until creamy. Once the yolk mixture is smooth, add the honey.

Blend the egg yolk mixture with the whisked egg whites and then start to slowly pour the mixture into the warm beer. Again, four hands are better than two for this, as you need to stir the beer continuously. Whatever you do, do not let the mixture get to hot, or you will end up with sweet scrambled eggs in your beer.

Once the eggs are incorporated into the beer, stir for a couple of minutes or so over a low heat.

Add the vanilla extract and brandy right at the end, just before turning the heat off. Cover the pan and leave for a few more minutes before serving – it should be warm but not boiling.

KEY INGREDIENTS

TWARÓG Fresh, white cheese available in most Polish shops. It may sometimes be replaced with ricotta, quark or another fresh cheese, such as the one you sometimes find in Turkish shops.

WHITE PEPPER This pepper is more delicate than black pepper and more common in Eastern European cooking. It's good to have both on hand, as they have completely different flavours.

MARJORAM This is an incredibly common dry herb in Poland, used in a wide variety of dishes.

DILL Dill is used so often in Polish cooking that cooks often have a box of frozen, ready chopped dill in the freezer. Fresh or frozen dill is preferable to the dried variety.

BREADCRUMBS My mum always has some on hand, she puts older bread in the oven to dry. After a few days of being warm and dry, you can grate it, push it through a sieve (a rather laborious process) or blitz it into fine breadcrumbs.

RAPESEED OIL We grow plenty of rapeseed in Poland and you can find this oil in most supermarkets. Back in the Communist days it was the only oil you could buy in Poland.

TOASTED BUCKWHEAT GROATS Now available in the World Food Sections of most supermarkets, as well as Polish shops. On the packet it will say *Kasza Gryczana, pra ona*, and the buckwheat groats will be dark brown in colour, as opposed to untoasted buckwheat groats, which are much lighter.

DRIED WILD MUSHROOMS In Poland everyone will have some dried mushrooms lying about that some trusted family member picked. *Prawidziwki* are probably the most popular they are called boletus in the West. You can buy dried mushrooms in Polish shops or delicatessens, and sometimes in the World Food section of the supermarket.

ALLSPICE In Poland this is called *ziele angielskie* – 'the English herb' – goodness knows why as this spice hails from Jamaica. This spice is crucial to Polish cooking. The dried berries are often added whole to classic dishes, though sometimes I prefer to use the spice in powder form to avoid the unpleasant sensation of biting into one.

SAREPSKA MUSTARD This is one of the ingredients you should buy if you are in a Polish shop, as it has a rather mild, sweet and unique taste. You can replace it with Dijon mustard for convenience, although the two do not taste alike and *sarepska* is always preferable in Polish cooking.

SAUERKRAUT You can buy sauerkraut everywhere nowadays, yet the quality varies. The sauerkraut you buy in a bag is superior to the sauerkraut you buy in a jar. You can also make your own sauerkraut quite easily. Back in the old days my mum remembers when they'd make whole barrels of it and children would stamp on the sauerkraut with their little bare feet.

GHERKINS If you are not keen on pickling your own, or you simply don't have 5 days to spare, then you can buy gherkins. There are a few different types. There are the hard gherkins pickled in vinegar called *ogórki konserwowe*, and the softer ones in brine *ogórki kiszone* or *ogórki kwaszone*. They taste completely different,

I prefer the latter generally called *ogórki konserwowe*. It's easier to buy the former, as they are popular in many cuisines, while the *kwaszone/kiszone* gherkins are available in Polish shops.

LOVAGE They say that when you add this herb to your lover's food that they will then love you forever. It's rare to find fresh lovage in the UK, though of course you can easily grow it, which is what I'd recommend. In Polish shops you should be able to get the dry variety, it's called *lubczyk*.

LEMON BALM A tangy, citrusy herb that is sold along with all the other fresh herbs in Polish supermarkets, though not so easily accessible worldwide. It has a calming effect when drunk as a tea/infusion. Another name for it is 'Melissa'. It is easy to grow in a window box.

HERRINGS Simple *Matjas* herrings are the ones we use in this book. You can get various *Matjas* herrings, in different sauces but when I refer to *Matjas* herrings, I mean the simplest ones. These are sold in a flat packet with a few herring fillets, just in oil. Back in the homelands, you used to get herrings straight out of the barrel and then soak them in milk or water to remove their salt. You can find these in every Polish shop.

DRIED POLISH SAUSAGES There are many dried sausages available in Polish shops and everyone has their own preference. In general, I suggest you buy *mysliwska* – 'Hunters' sausage' for all cooking, grilling and frying purposes. It's widely available and very versatile.

ZASMAŻKA (ROUX) This is a base we commonly use for many vegetables and sauces in Polish cooking. We use approximately equal amounts of butter and flour. We melt the butter and then add flour, stirring all the time.

STOCKS It's always useful to have some good stock available: ideally both a meat and a vegetable one. Make some in advance then keep it in the fridge for up to 5 days, or freeze it. Otherwise, buy the best quality stock you can find.

{Vegetable stock} Cook 1 carrot, 1 parsnip, 1 onion, ½ peeled celeriac (celery root), 2 celery stalks (with leaves) and 1 bay leaf in the largest pot you can find, covered in water for about 3 hours. Add large pinch of sea salt and 2 peppercorns half way through cooking time.

{Chicken stock} Cook all the ingredients that you used for vegetable stock but also add a few piece of chicken with the bones still in.

SAUERKRAUT Chop the cabbage very finely, place it in a bowl and cover it with a tablespoon of salt. Massage the seasoning into the cabbage with your hands then use your equipment of choice to pound the cabbage gently for a long period of time – perhaps 15–20 minutes, or until its juices are released. Then add half a grated carrot or a teaspoon of caraway seeds. The cabbage is then transferred to a (previously sterilised) jar. Use something heavy (like a rock or can) to press the cabbage down, making sure that it's fully submerged in its own juices. After 3 days, taste the cabbage: if you like this lightly fermented sauerkraut then close your jar and place it in the fridge. However, if you would like a stronger flavour (as I do) then allow the cabbage to ferment for 5 days.

LILAC AND ROSE JAMS These are two traditional jams that I use in this book. Rose petal jam can be bought quite easily in Poland (and in some, better stocked Polish shops in other countries), but lilac jam is rare.

We use a pestle and mortar to grind the flower petals with sugar, until the grains disintegrate. We then place it in a sterilised jar, close it and cook it in the same water you sterilised the jar in for about 2 hours. Keep topping the boiling water up as it evaporates. When you take the jars out allow them to cool upside down.

GINGERBREAD

Making proper gingerbread – the sort you could build a small house with – takes some time: 3–4 days for the dough to mature before baking. The other secret to a beautiful gingerbread is the spice mix. It's like your own special garam masala blend, except this one is for baking. You can, of course, alter the proportions of spices to suit your own preferences – as mine is quite spicy.

FOR THE DOUGH

300g (10½ oz/2½ cups) plain (all-purpose) flour
200ml (7 fl oz/⅔ cups) runny honey
50g soft unsalted butter
1 teaspoon bicarbonate of soda (baking soda)
1 egg

FOR THE SPICE MIX

2 teaspoons ground ginger
½ teaspoon ground cinnamon
½ teaspoon allspice
½ teaspoon ground nutmeg
¼ teaspoon salt
¼ teaspoon ground black pepper
4–5 cardamom pods
2–3 cloves
1 star anise

Make the spice mix first – I always use pestle and mortar but you can use a coffee grinder or blender. Throw the cardamom shells away once the seeds have popped out.

Combine the ingredients for the dough with the spice mix and knead together for 5–6 minutes, until a soft ball is formed. Cover your dough ball with a clean, damp tea towel (dish towel) and place in the fridge for 3 days.

After 3 days, preheat the oven to 180°C (350°F/gas 4). Line a baking tray with baking paper (parchment paper). Remove the ball from the fridge and knead it again, on a floured surface, until it softens once again for about 10–12 minutes.

Roll the dough out to a ½ cm (¼ in) thickness on a lightly floured surface. Cut out the shapes of your choosing and place them on a baking tray lined with baking paper (parchment paper). Bake for 12–15 minutes on 180°C (350°F/gas 4). Allow to cool before eating. Best eaten on the following day and do save some for breadcrumbs.

INDEX

BIBLIOGRAPHY

W Staropolskiej Kuchni i Przy Polskim Stole
Maria Lemnis and Henryk Vitry,
Wydawnictwo Interpress Warsawa, 1989

Sekrety Kuchmistrzowskie Stanisława Czernieckiego. Przepisy z Najstarszej Polskiej Książki Kucharskiej z 1682 Roku
Jarosław Dumanowski, Andrzej Pawlas, Jerzy Poznański
Muzeum Pałac w Wilanowie, 2012

Sekret Kucharski – Co Jadano w Soplicowie
Hanna Szymanderska
Warszawa : Prószyński i S-ka, 1999.

Encyclopaedia of Polish cuisine : 2400 traditional & modern recipes
Hanna Szymanderska.
Warszawa : Wydawnictwo "Rea", 2006.

Polska Wigilia
Hanna Szymanderska.
Warszawa : Muza SA, 2000.

Kuchnia Polska: Potrawy Regionalne
Hanna Szymanderska
Świat Książki So. z.o.o., Warszawa 2010

Polska Kuchnia Myśliwska
Hanna Szymanderska.
Warszawa : Muza SA, 2002

Książka Kucharska Jako Tekst
Waldemar Żarski
Wrocław : Wydawnictwo. Uniwersytetu Wrocławskiego, 2008

Cooking the Polish way
Danuta Zamojska-Hutchins
Minneapolis : Lerner, c1984

Food and Drink in Medieval Poland
Maria Dembińska, University of Pennsylvania Press, 2016

The Art of Polish Cooking
Alina Żerańska, Doubleday, 1968

Pan Tadeusz or The Last Foray in Lithuania
Adam Mickiewicz, translation by Kenneth R. Mackenzie, The Polish Cultural Foundation, 1990

The Comic Stories
Anton Chekhov
Ivan R. Dee Publisher, 1999

The Siren
Anton Chekhov
1887

ACKNOWLEDGMENTS

Firstly, I would like to thank everyone at Quadrille for producing this book that I love, especially Sarah Lavelle, Helen Lewis, Romilly Morgan and Claire Rochford. I am also immensely grateful to the photographer, Laura Edwards, who along with the very talented Marina Filippelli and Tabitha Hawkins, created such lovely images of my food.

My biggest thank you has to go to my mum, Teresa, without whose herculean efforts this book would not have been possible. She kept me going. Thank you also to my dad, Kajetan, for his unwavering belief in me. Thank you to my partner, Yasin Salazar, and my little brother, Robert, for both of their moral and practical support and for editing me so vehemently when it was needed. To Lili Weston, for the beautiful wild flowers on that hot day.

In Poland, I would also like to thank Julia and Andrzej Jendrych, who are always willing to help and my darling Magda Pałkus for our food chats and inspiration. Indeed, I am grateful to my entire extended family – aunties, uncles and my cousin Wera – who have all contributed in one way or another. Thank you also to my dear friend, Anna Van Praagh, who planted the seed. And a very, very big thank you to my agent, Isabel Atherton, for taking me on and making this book happen.

Publishing Director: Sarah Lavelle
Creative Director: Helen Lewis
Editor: Romilly Morgan
Design and Art Direction: Claire Rochford
Photographer: Laura Edwards
Photographer's Assistant: Kendal Noctor
Illustrator: Holly MacDonald
Food Stylist: Marina Filippelli
Food Stylist's Assistant: Becks Wilkinson
Prop Stylist: Tabitha Hawkins
Production: Vincent Smith and Emily Noto

First published in 2016 by
Quadrille Publishing
Pentagon House
52–54 Southwark Street
London SE1 1UN
www.quadrille.co.uk
www.quadrille.com

Quadrille is an imprint of Hardie Grant
www.hardiegrant.com.au

Cataloguing in Publication Data: a catalogue record for this book is available from the British Library.

ISBN: 978 184949 726 8

Printed in China